WOKE
PARENTING

Raising Intersectional Feminist, Empathic, Engaged, and Generally Non-Shitty Kids while Still Having a Life

FAITH G. HARPER PHD, LPC–S, ACS, ACN & BONNIE SCOTT MA, MS, LPC

MICROCOSM PUBLISHING
Portland, Ore

WOKE PARENTING

Raising Intersectional Feminist, Empathic, Engaged, and Generally Non-Shitty Kids while Still Having a Life

© 2021 Faith G Harper and Bonnie Scott

© This edition Microcosm Publishing 2021

First edition - 3,000 copies - October 26, 2021

ISBN 978-1-62106-939-3

This is Microcosm #443

Edited by Lydia Rogue

Designed by Joe Biel

Cover by Lindsey Cleworth

To join the ranks of high-class stores that feature Microcosm titles, talk to your local rep: In the U.S. COMO (Atlantic), FUJII (Midwest), BOOK TRAVELERS WEST (Pacific), TURNAROUND (Europe), UTP/MANDA (Canada), NEW SOUTH (Australia/New Zealand), GPS in Asia, Africa, India, South America, and other countries, or FAIRE in the gift trade.

For a catalog, write or visit:

Microcosm Publishing

2752 N Williams Ave.

Portland, OR 97227

https://microcosm.pub/WokeParenting

Did you know that you can buy our books directly from us at sliding scale rates? Support a small, independent publisher and pay less than Amazon's price at www.Microcosm.Pub

Global labor conditions are bad, and our roots in industrial Cleveland in the 70s and 80s made us appreciate the need to treat workers right. Therefore, our books are MADE IN THE USA.

MICROCOSM · PUBLISHING

MICROCOSM PUBLISHING is Portland's most diversified publishing house and distributor with a focus on the colorful, authentic, and empowering. Our books and zines have put your power in your hands since 1996, equipping readers to make positive changes in their lives and in the world around them. Microcosm emphasizes skill-building, showing hidden histories, and fostering creativity through challenging conventional publishing wisdom with books and bookettes about DIY skills, food, bicycling, gender, self-care, and social justice. What was once a distro and record label was started by Joe Biel in his bedroom and has become among the oldest independent publishing houses in Portland, OR. We are a politically moderate, centrist publisher in a world that has inched to the right for the past 80 years.

CONTENTS

INTRODUCTION

Welcome friends! We are so excited you're reading our book.

If you like it, that is.

If you don't, we now feel really bad that you spent some dollar bills and time on it.

Ahem. But *anyway*.

Maybe you already have kids in your home or life, whether you donated genetic material to their conception or not. Or maybe you are preparing for a nugget or maybe you're preparing for that part of your life. Either way, we feel hopeful you'll find some ideas here that will be helpful to you in raising and supporting the kids around you to be thoughtful, progressive, and inclusive. As adults, we are working toward a more egalitarian world; we also need to build the scaffolding for future progress and safety for all. That sturdiness of this scaffolding relies on us teaching our kids about the realities of the world and the possibilities, too.

The common phrase "there's no such thing as other people's kids" is a guiding principle of this book. What affects one kid affects them all in some way. The decisions that get made around health care, education, libraries, school lunch programming . . . those affect all kids, so there's no such thing as other people's kids. What affects yours also affects ours and vice versa. It means we treat all kids the way we wish our own kids could be treated: with kindness, thoughtfulness, and foresight. It takes all of us, looking out for all of them, to make real and lasting changes in society. So when we talk about "parenting" in the context of this book, really what we are talking about is the common denominator of guiding and caring about young people and their futures. Maybe you're a bio parent, a stepparent, an adoptive or foster parent, a cool auntie, a youth director, a teacher, a bus driver . . . You're a person who has responsibility to and for young people.

The ideas and topics in this book are a compilation of conversations with our own kids, their friends, our friends, our clients, and our own families, in addition to memories of our own understanding of feminism and family. We are not experts in feminist theory and we know that feminism means a lot of things to a lot of people. Feminism and progressivism are full of contradictions, and sometimes there's no "right" answer to the big questions.

When we first started this project as a series of zines, we wanted it to reflect the newer, more intersectional feminism rather than the one we grew up with. In 2017, the word "woke" was added to the Merriam-Webster Dictionary, defining it as "aware of and actively attentive to important facts and issues (especially issues of racial and social justice)." The term is much older than that, of course. It was first used in a 1962 *New York Times* essay by novelist William Melvin Kelley. It started to really gain traction after Erykah Badu used "I stay woke" as a hook in her song "Master Teacher" in 2008.

As we are publishing this in 2021, the term has been co-opted from *SNL* skits to the antics of suburban teens on TikTok. But the original use of the term still has a deep power. It may have been co-opted, but it can't be corrupted. Because woke means *we don't look away*. From any of it. Our mandate as humans is to be in and of this world.

The individual we know as the Buddha was a Hindu prince named Siddhārtha Gautama. He was protected from all pain and sickness and brokenness in the world by his parents Śuddhodana and Māyādevī. But he awakened to the fact that being protected from the world didn't save anyone in the end, even him. We all need to be in and of this world, and raise kids that live the same. This is the only way to save us.

That makes it sound far simpler than it is in reality, of course. The ground shifts quickly, both in our personal lives and in the wider sphere. Over the course of writing this book, Bonnie's kid grew from a salty toddler to a salty elementary school student. Faith's kids grew up and moved out to lives of their own, and it happened so quickly. Add to that feeling of "I blinked and now all their shoes are too small" the idea of keeping up with a quickly shifting cultural experience and wow; it can be a dizzying challenge. There's a lot to navigate between changing bodies, changing needs, changing emotions (parents' and kids'), changing climate, and changing politics. Parenting asks for our best selves, and that's all we can give in the uncertainty around us.

We hope this book gives you a framework for talking about your own intersectional feminism with kids in your life and helps you create a space for discussion and growth. Don't wait for your kid to get to Gender Studies 101 in college before they've heard these ideas or had a chance to work for justice and progress.

RAISING
WOKE KIDS

When Faith (Gen-X af) and Bonnie (Xennial who fits in nowhere) were growing up, all the world asked for or expected of our parental units was that they generally kept us alive. Most parents didn't take on the task of paying attention to the emotional needs of their kids back then. Everyone was expected to just toughen up. And those same parents (now grandparents) often grumble that these kids today are coddled and bratty instead of seeing the possibility that these young people are growing up in unprecedented times while navigating the inheritance of everything all the previous generations got wrong. They deserve a fighting chance, and having a nurturing home environment is the very best tool for doing so. Caring is not coddling, all right?

So this is our list of the shit kids need to have a fighting chance at success when they fly the nest. These are some ideas of how you begin to incorporate a kid and their needs into your established adult life (while facing the fact that you may not feel like the adult in the room yet). See this as a guide to creating a culture of support and openness in your home and with your kids so they have a better chance of growing up to be collaborative people who can carry their own physical and emotional labor. Whether your kids are newborn, basically grown, or somewhere in between, it's never too late to start shifting your approach to them in order to support their emotional and relational growth.

How to Navigate Woke Parenting When You Weren't Raised Woke

We would wager there are few among us who were truly raised woke. Our families are as varied as we are, and each family does the best they can with what they've got. Particularly in the U.S., we are all products of a pretty toxic culture based on fear, scarcity, conformity, and misinformation. A culture that supports ideas of "bootstrapping" and meritocracy, and thinks of differences as something to be mocked instead of celebrated. Because we all breathe this toxic air, sometimes we breathe it back out. So if you weren't raised to actively question yourself and your beliefs, you might be breathing out those toxic fumes more often than you realize. You might be acting in ways that are hurtful to others, even if your intention is to cause no harm. You may be planting some of these ideas in your own kids' brains because you're not questioning parts of your identity or belief system. If you want to be a woke parent, that means you need to be ready to be uncomfortable. You're going to have to question your beliefs and look for the places in which they are based on falsehoods that have been passed to you from patriarchy itself. You're going to have to be ready to take responsibility for those hurts, and you'll have to process the shame that comes with hurting someone. That might mean having some tough conversations with people you've hurt, and listening to them with an open heart and a desire to understand other people's experiences of you. And that's all hard work and it can feel much easier to turn away from that discomfort and go with the flow. Please resist that temptation; your discomfort is very unlikely to kill you. You can feel it even though it might be painful or gross. It's a hard thing that's totally worth it because processing that discomfort and finding a new, more woke way forward will benefit you and your kids and your community in ways you can't imagine.

It may be helpful to think about your own youth experience. What conversations were in the media? What are ideas that felt like they were in the bloodstream of your family, church, or school? How were the adults who were in charge of the culture then maybe not doing as good a job as you would like to do now when it comes to tough conversations or ideas?

There are books and podcasts and guided journals out there that can help you process your internalized biases toward yourself and others around you. We've listed some of our favorites at the end of the book, but also suggest you ask people whom you respect for the names of resources they have found most useful. Between us writing and you reading, amazing work will become available that didn't exist in time for us to mention in these pages. Or we plain just didn't know about it.

You may not be able to avoid breathing those toxic fumes, but you can actively work to transform them into fresh air before you breathe them out again. Your kids can breathe that fresher air and be more primed for self-reflection and compassion. If you're choosing to be a woke parent even if you weren't raised that way, you're taking a stand and beginning to heal generations of trauma and pain. That's definitely not easy but it is brave as fuck.

Now's the time to be really compassionate toward yourself and the you that held the ideas and biases you're examining. The process of learning, growing, and integrating new understandings of yourself and others is a constant process. We don't want to be dishonest about the moments that came before this one—we thought, felt, and experienced those moments, even if they were far from ideal. But the idea of learning and growing means that we can own those previous moments without shame driving the narrative. And when you're mindful of your own trauma, processing, and growth, it's beneficial to the kids you're guiding. It means you're engaging in learning, you're making thoughtful decisions, and you're showing them how to be critically compassionate with themselves as well.

Create a Safe Home for Feelings of All Kinds

As parents, we have our own triggers and traumas, and sometimes we avoid anything related to them because it feels gross to be triggered and worked up. And the impact of that is a home where some feelings are okay but some are not. We've had so many clients who talk about when they were growing up, there was no acceptable way to be mad, or sad, or maybe even too happy, depending on the triggers of the parents. If we as parents aren't aware of our triggers, depression, and anxiety (you know, all that baggage shit from our own lives), we may be subconsciously sending the message to our kids that some feelings aren't okay. When our kids inevitably feel those "not okay" feelings, then we are losing our shit on them, or teaching them they gotta stuff that shit down because home isn't a place for that particular feeling.

So first; what's a trigger? That is a small word that leads to a big impact on people and can be defined in a lot of ways. The classic definition is associated with a trauma response and is a hallmark of a post-traumatic stress disorder diagnosis. That's anything, including an event, memory, sensation, that results in an intense emotional response, regardless of your mood. That response will be involuntary, intense, and can feel crippling. As language tends to do, the word has morphed from the classic definition to mean anything from that PTSD-level of reaction to anything that makes us feel uncomfortable. Defining the word and experience of trigger for yourself will mean you need to (1) notice your intense emotional reactions, and (2) be able to pay attention to what aspects of your life or interactions bring about those intense emotional reactions. Are you having a response to a traumatic memory or reliving a traumatic moment? Are you feeling envious, angry, or shameful? Does the response look like fear, anger, shallow breathing, crying, tearfulness, or avoidance?

We cannot avoid all of the situations or interactions that may emotionally trigger us. Therefore, it's our responsibility to examine the times we've felt those emotional responses to understand what was activated for us and find healthy coping skills to help us manage the responses we experience.

Set out to make your home a place that's safe for feelings of all kinds. The big ones, the confusing ones, the hurtful ones. Home is where we can explore those feelings in a safe space. If you're triggered and need help to move past that, you might want to talk about that feeling with a trusted friend or a therapist. If you're not sure what your triggers are, start by noticing when you feel any kind of "out of control" feeling. All feelings are okay, but everyone needs to practice acceptable ways of showing them. That means you need to have some conversations about what's okay in your home and what isn't.

We know, yet one more thing that we are responsible for doing in order to not ruin our kids. But this is one of those conversations that makes life way easier for everyone in the house, especially the parent-people. It's the best way to be proactive about addressing the more manageable mental health issues in hopes they will not become huge, untenable ones. Start with pregame convos, setting the standard that these are not elephant-in-the-room, closed topics of conversation. Then, when life gets really spiky, it will be easier to speak truth to pain. And as matter of factly as "the trash needs to go out to the curb" or "wash your hands, dinner will be on the table in three minutes."

These conversations can happen at any time with yourself or between you and the other adults in your home. You may notice it's time to start these conversations if your home feels tense or anxious. What's the vibe in your house? Does it feel safe to feel all kinds of feelings or is it feeling a little restricted? Start to answer these questions by listing some of your own feelings and the ways you might recognize them in yourself and also the ways you show them to others. Ask yourself "When I feel happy, how do I know I feel happy? How do I show my happiness to people around me?" and continue going through emotions until you've got a solid list. It could look like:

- Happy: I know I'm happy when I feel lightness in my chest or a smile on my face. I like to show my happiness to others by smiling, telling them with words, or throwing confetti.

- Sad: I know I'm sad when my body feels heavy or I feel the pressure of tears behind my eyes. I don't like other people to see my sadness so I am not sure how I want to show that feeling.

- Hangry: I know I'm hangry when everything inconvenient feels like a huge hurdle. I want to recognize hangry for myself and take care of myself instead of showing that irritation to my family.

It may be helpful to use a tool like an emotion wheel. It's a visual representation that gives you a lot of words for emotions, and that increased vocabulary can be really useful if you're new to exploring emotions.

Once you've got your own list, then you can ask the other people in your home to make those lists as well. You can include kids of all ages, and you can be creative in that process. You know your kids. Maybe they are glad to make a list. Maybe smaller kids need to draw or use modeling clay. Maybe teens need to make a playlist. The process is really just to show that you're a family that's open to talking about feelings.

Plan a time to sit and talk about your lists a little bit as a group. Learn more about the inner world of the people with whom you share your life and space. Decide together how you want to communicate feelings, what's okay, and what's not. In Bonnie's home, it's okay to feel angry, but it's not okay to slam doors. It is okay to say "Ughhh, I need a minute!" and then go spend a few minutes in a bedroom or bathroom. There are no limits on feelings, but the actions used to show them need boundaries. Those boundaries will be different in every home, and may require some conversations or workshopping to make sure everyone is feeling safe. For some of us who are healing from trauma, things like loud voices or slamming doors may be very frightening. For others, a frosty silence may be the most frightening sound of all. It's important to talk about how each person in your home responds to emotional cues so that everyone can regulate their responses for a more peaceful home.

When someone in your home is triggered, which happens even in the most thoughtful homes, it can be helpful to have a "take a break" agreement. The average person needs about twenty to thirty minutes to regroup after the flooding feeling of anger or fear triggers. That twenty minutes is the time to tap into coping skills, self-care, reflection, and other return-to-safety processes. It is not the time to plan a loud and forceful argument about why everyone else in this exchange sucks. It's a time to take care of yourself so you can return to the discussion, event, or interaction in a way that's regulated and peaceful, setting everyone up for success.

Help Kids Find a Coping Skill and Don't Take it Away

The ability to self-soothe and handle tough feelings or situations is both a lifelong skill and an ongoing process. We all have things that help us feel safer, calmer, and cared for, and we can help our kids find those activities by giving them options and ideas to try.

We can watch what they do naturally and offer it as a coping option. We innately seek homeostasis (unless trauma has hacked our ability to do so to bits). You'll see these behaviors in the way a baby cuddles up to a trusted person and falls asleep. Or a toddler who, upon finding their favorite toy, shows visible relief on their little face. An elementary kid who always looks for the cat when she's feeling a little sad. An adolescent who video chats with their friends when they are stressed about homework. As you're watching kids regulate themselves, offer that feedback. It might sound like, "I can see you feel a little more calm now that you've found your stuffy. Your stuffy helps you feel comfortable." And you will see them visibly calm down, have fun, and feel better. You may struggle to identify those behaviors happening in real time. That's totally normal. If you haven't been able to identify self-soothing behaviors, you can also identify some things that you know help you feel more regulated and offer those as suggestions. A little bit of time in the sun, some alone time, a favorite song, a comfy blanket, writing in a journal; there's a long list of possible comforts. Communicate that these are things to try, not punishments to bear. And they don't have to continue any activity that doesn't help. You're providing a valuable service to help your kids recognize those possibilities and learn to use those behaviors to return to a calm baseline.

And that's important . . . but then you might feel tempted to use that as leverage to help improve behavior. But coping skills should never be taken away as part of a punishment. Faith tells this story of herself when training parents and other people who work with kiddos. Her son's (Kid #2) anger coping skill was to go outside and throw his football at the big tree in the back. The tree didn't take it personally and the physical exercise and repetitive movement was an important part of getting himself re-regulated.

At one point they were fighting about something. No idea what, because his 15th year was a series of chaotic moments with brief interludes of calm before the next storm came crashing to shore. Faith and Kid #2 were going at it, and he asked to be excused to go outside. Faith, mad and not done being mad, said "no." Kid #2 reminded her, "Hey, you said if I ever needed to calm down I could go outside and throw my football at the tree." First of all, bless his head for advocating for himself instead of ramping up more because he was straight-up, dead-on right-as-fuck. He was trying to activate his safety plan and Faith's job right then and there was to let him.

But first of all, she had to say she was sorry for saying no, and praise him for doing all the right things in that situation. Apologizing to our kids in the ways that adults never apologized to us when we were kids is hugely important in modeling accountability. We're gonna talk about this again later, of course, because we do enjoy saying things seven different ways nine different times, it's a habit born of being therapists!

We have a tendency, as parents, to desperately try to find the things that matter to our kids and use them to leverage the behavioral expectations we have for them. I mean, really. We're trying not to beat their asses . . . and grounding them feels like the same punishment for us as it is for them because then they're stuck in our houses glaring at us. But we have to remember to not take away the shit that helps hold them together. Their sports, their extracurriculars, their quiet time in their room, their music, their tree-and-football routine, even their phones and electronics. We spent all that time helping them curate healthy coping skills and activities to support their positive humaning. Taking that away from them is really fucked because it undermines their ability to self-regulate, which is the whole thing we were trying to teach them to do. We gotta stop that shit. Have a separate set of consequences that have nothing to do with the coping/calm down skills you're helping your kid build.

Don't Have Power Struggles

You want a more peaceful home, yes? A place where people are respectful and working together and always replacing the toilet paper correctly? Of course you do. Wouldn't it be way easier to achieve if everyone you live with would just do what you say to do already? Of course it would. But, slavish subservience is not the goal. What you're really seeking is a peaceful home where people are respectful and work together and replace the toilet paper correctly, but those people can think for themselves and do things at their own pace and even have their own way of replacing the toilet paper. (Even though we all know the only way is with the loose end coming over the top, obviously.)

So don't seek out submission. Don't let yourself get wrapped up in winning a battle with your children because you want the win. We get it; parenting is hard and doesn't necessarily come with a lot of wins. And kids' lives are hard and don't necessarily come with a lot of wins. It's a frequent battle between parents and kids because everyone wants the win and stubbornness comes in full force. But if you want a peaceful and collaborative home, the goal can't always be the "win;" the goal needs to be finding a way together.

This doesn't mean that you have to acquiesce every time. It does mean taking a less emotional approach in order to focus on, and shape the behavior in question. Have you ever had the type of experience where someone else wanted you to do something their way *and* be happy about it *and* properly ashamed for not seeing it or doing it the way they wanted in the first place? The fuck is up with that, are we right? You said you'd do what they wanted, but do you need to fall on your sword in the process??? That's an experience based in ideas of hierarchy and power differential, and we don't want to be preparing our kids to fit into that power structure in other parts of their lives. They need us to show them another way to interact and accomplish tasks.

When it comes to something that might become a battle, take a deep breath. Focus on your end goal and recognize there might be more than just your way of reaching that goal. Let's say you need the compost taken out every day, and you're assigning it as a task for your kid. The goal is getting the stinky coffee grounds and bell pepper stems out of your kitchen, yes? It doesn't really matter if it happens right after school or just before bed. You might have a preference (and obviously that's fine!) but don't power struggle over something like that, just focus on the end goal of having an empty compost container.

If you're one of those people who has to feel like you've won, work on ways that you and your kid can win together. Bonnie's husband is a champ at this approach, which is: decide for yourself the minimum level of acquiescence you need from your kid to feel like you've won. Then step it up one notch and ask your kid for that. If they agree to that, *bonus*. But, with this method, if you need space to negotiate, you've got it.

Avoiding these power struggles is another important aspect of keeping the people in your house regulated. You'll have fewer arguments and blowups because the overall stress feels lower and everyone is managing their own central nervous systems and stress responses. That's a valuable skill for life and helps kids build resilience and mindfulness—there's a solid parenting win that actually matters.

Keep Your End Goals in Mind

It's sometimes wild to realize that you're shaping this smaller human into some kind of bigger, adult human. But you are doing that! And that's a big responsibility and you want to do it in a goal-focused way. Think about what kind of adult you're producing to give over to the world and keep that at the forefront of your interactions and discussions. Are you building this kid to be an adult automaton? Or an adult who follows rules and guidelines thoughtfully? Is what you are fighting about something that is going to be a fundamentally defining aspect of their humanity? It might be, if we are talking about bullying, or keeping your word, or being kind and empathic.

Those are the fights worth fighting.

It may not be a fight worth fighting if we are talking about broccoli.

Faith was chatting with a client who was fighting with their ex about their son's dinner time routine. Ex wanted a clean plate. Client had a courtesy-bite rule. Client wasn't getting steamrolled by Kiddo, but also wasn't playing Miss Hannigan, the antagonist from *Annie*. She said to Faith, "When I think about all the things

I value and want to see my child grow up to be as an adult, 'good eater' isn't anywhere on that list."

Faith and Bonnie love that perspective. Kiddo needs appropriate nutrition. Kiddo needs to be open to experiences and willing to experiment and challenge himself. Kiddo needs to respect the effort that people put into meal preparation.

Kiddo does not need to love roasted Brussels sprouts. And setting up a fight over Brussels sprouts is fertile grounds for resentments at best, and eating disorders at worst.

What are your parenting end goals? Is what you're feeling annoyed about in this moment an important step on that path? Or can you show some grace and flexibility and let it go?

Boundaries All Over the Fucking Place

Kids need boundaries to help keep them safe. You need boundaries to help keep you safe. Kids will push and push; they need to know where the clear limits are. Laying out clear boundaries helps you create reprimands, corrections, and conversations that are productive, instead of feeling violated when someone crosses a boundary you didn't know you had or needed.

Whatever boundaries you set need to be reasonable, clearly stated, and might need some explanation. For Bonnie, an important boundary is limiting snacks after school. This is hardly arbitrary, but it can seem that way to a four- or five-year-old. So, Bonnie has explained to her daughter that snacks after school are fun, but dinner is happening in 45 minutes and if she eats a bunch of snacks, her tummy won't be hungry, and then she'll act a fool during dinner. It's nicer for everyone to sit down to dinner and feel genuine hunger in their tummies and joy at having food to share.

Boundaries don't make you some kind of buzzkill parent. They make you the parent all the kids want to be around, because they know where they stand and what to expect. You're like the cord attached to the bungee jumper.

Conversations about boundaries will be ongoing and fluid. Some boundaries people innately know they need and can be laid out easily. Some boundaries people may not recognize they need until they feel disrespected and realize they need a clear boundary. Sometimes boundaries change over time, based on people's preferences, emotional availability, or changing perceptions of safety. Some boundaries look different for different people in your life. You might be willing to loan out your lawn mower to the neighbor on the right, because you trust they will respect your property and boundaries, but the neighbor on the left will get nowhere near your stuff because they don't have the same respect.

Whatever the situation, teach kids to lay out boundaries calmly and kindly, yet firmly. Offer them some language to try, like "I see you want a hug but I am not in the mood right now," or "You hugged me without asking first and I felt a little uncomfortable. Please ask first next time," or even "Last time we saw each other I was not in the mood for hugs, but I feel like hugs are okay today. Would you like a hug?" Allow them to practice that language with you so they find something that feels comfortable and authentic. Boundaries that are founded in empathy and are communicated in kindness are very likely to be respected. So one way to keep the conversation about boundaries in the forefront is to be empathetic to your kids' needs.

Boundaries often come into conflict in relationships and it's important to teach our kids (and remind ourselves) that all boundaries are our everyday expressions of consent. And they aren't always going to match up nicely with how everyone else navigates the world. Having boundaries that are flexible (as opposed to super rigid or super permeable) is a helpful part of that process, as is the empathy mentioned above. There is no magic answer to how to handle conflicting boundaries, but it's amazing what we can resolve when maintaining connection.

The more we can approach our kids with empathy, the calmer our relationships can feel. It helps to put yourself in the place of your kid; think about how it feels to be little, and learning, while simultaneously sure you are capable of anything while not actually knowing how to do things. When you feel frustrated, imagine how your kid might be feeling and how you wish people would respond to you when you feel that way. If you were learning how to put your shoes on the right feet, how to drive a stick shift in traffic, or how to get all your homework done on time . . . you'd hope for kindness, compassion, and understanding. Think about that and offer it to your kids: "If I were you, I would feel [insert feeling word here] and I would want to know [A, B, and C] before moving forward. What do you need?"

Parenting from a headspace of empathy means being present and thoughtful. It means we avoid default or snarky answers to questions or requests. Take some time to examine your default answers to things. One day, Bonnie and her husband offered their daughter a "Yes Day" and told her that she could choose all the activities for the day, and no one would say "no" as long as what she wanted was safe and affordable. It was a super fun day, involving pancakes and a trip to the bookstore, but it was also an interesting exercise in setting boundaries, avoiding power struggles, and noticing how often their answer to her requests is a default "no." That part was eye-opening. What are your default answers? What's your motivation for those answers? Are you building a respectful relationship with your kids or would you like to make some different moves? Connect with your own feelings and needs and make your decisions less default reactions and more of a thoughtful process.

Praise the Behaviors You Want to See More Of

There is a form of structured, evidence-based therapy called Parent-Child Interaction Therapy (PCIT). It's brilliant with younger kids who have serious behavioral issues. One of the things that it teaches parents to do (using play as the interaction format) is to differentiate labeled and unlabeled praise and use labeled praise as much as possible.

The idea is to be specific in your praise. Instead of saying "you're such a great kid!" all the time (not that saying that is a bad thing at all), it is focusing on a level of specificity of, "You did such a great job bringing your plate into the kitchen without me having to even remind you. I really appreciate that."

When Faith was training in PCIT, she commented on one of her bonus kid's fancy way of folding the napkins at family dinner. "Wow, that looks really cool. Thank you for taking the time to make the dinner table look so nice for everyone. That was above and beyond your job to set the table." Damned if that kiddo didn't fold the napkins fancy for family dinners for the next two years.

The idea is to use this as a genuine way to praise and build up the actions you want to see. Sometimes this gets twisted into a snarky approach, like "Well, look who finally graced us with her presence this afternoon," or "Oh look! He does, in fact, know how to use a washing machine," but that is not an authentic use of praise. It feels bad to people on the receiving end and it's not at all in the spirit of praising the characteristics we want to see. Yes, we feel snarky sometimes but that kind of "praise" is really a form of punishment directed at the behavior we want to encourage rather than discourage.

Using authentic praise is a universal tool. It works not just with small kiddos, but also large and smelly ones. It works pretty damn well on adults, too, whether they work with you or live in your house (or both).

Let Them Voice Their Opinion, Even if They Don't Get a Vote

Let's talk about valuing our kids' opinions, wants, and desires. Because they do have them. And those opinions and desires can be very strong, but you may not know about any of that if you're not inviting kids into the decision-making process in your home.

Faith and her co-parent team would often collect all the kiddos when there was a big family decision to be made and ask for their input. This was always prefaced with the following: "You aren't actually getting to make the final decision. This isn't a family vote type of decision like what desserts to make for Thanksgiving. But we genuinely want to know your thoughts on the subject. They will help us inform the decision we make, and at the very least, prepare us for your response to them." Bonus is that kids will have some awareness of the decisions being made that impact their lives, it gives them some mental preparation time, and they don't feel like they are being tossed around at the whim of the adults around them.

Sometimes our kiddos had a very good rationale that absolutely influenced the route we took. Sometimes not. But then we could have a proactive conversation about our process. As in "Hey, Kid

#2, we totally get why you wanted X, Y, and Z, but we ended up choosing A, B, and C, and here is why."

The decisions we make as parents affect our families as a whole. Sometimes those decisions are mundane and the consequences minor, but everyone in the family has an opinion. It's so easy to ask kids for their input on weekly meal planning, what they want in their lunches, what they want to do on a Saturday. Some decisions are much bigger, and we might not want as much decision power to go to kids, like if we should move, or change jobs, or how to celebrate the life of a loved one who's died. But from the day-to-day to the once-in-a-lifetime decisions, all family members will be affected, and it's respectful to at least ask for input and have those discussions before the adults make the final plan.

Kids already don't have a ton of autonomy or control. We drive them places. We buy their clothes. We take them to school. Every action that happens around them affects them and their lives. But they don't necessarily have a lot of power in these areas. And it can feel pretty shitty to feel the effects of decisions in your life that you had little control over and just have to live with. It's unfair to our kids for them to have to feel this as often as they do. Including them in discussions about decisions and changes can go a long way in lessening that feeling of loss of control and lack of influence that already is inherent in childhood. Faith's dad was career military, and she remembers her parents were making the decision about him either being stationed in Korea for a year while they stayed stateside or stationed in Germany for three years and they would go with them. Now Faith has always been a slightly anxious human, but this didn't make things worse, instead, it allowed her time to think about both of those options and have some mental preparation for both which felt far less shitty, even at age nine, than receiving decrees from the adult people about what was coming next in her life.

Let Your Kids into Your Public Living Space

In the same vein as building feelings of influence and autonomy, the idea of sharing your public living spaces is powerful. Kids got added to your established life, right? To make physical space for them in your home is to make emotional space for them in your life.

This is a subtle way of showing your kids that they belong in your home and your life, they aren't just people who live here because state law has determined that's the plan. Let your children claim space in common living areas, not just their own room. This doesn't mean letting the fucking contents of their toy chest throw up on your living room carpet. It means letting them discuss art and art placement, and letting them have their own tchotchke space as well. Faith had a friend with a display cabinet, the bottom shelf left empty for her girls. They were allowed to use that shelf (the reachable one for them) to display whichever of their toys and lovies were important to them, in the same place mom displayed hers.

We love this. *Love this.* Faith's kiddos having their art in shared spaces gave them an appreciation for art and made them far better at caring for their shared space. Though her son will remind her frequently, "Don't forget that's mine and it's going with me," about pieces in the house. They have similar taste so shit's gonna get real as he gets closer to having his own abode.

The more welcome your kids feel in your home, the more they feel they belong there, the more calm and attached they will feel.

That emotional safety can go a long way for all of you to avoid losing your shit on each other.

There's power in feeling influence over your physical surroundings. It feels good for our opinions to be sought out, heard, and valued. Something as simple as "Do you like this family photo in this frame or that one?" is a minor question, but kids feel good when we solicit their opinions. When people ask what we think, we feel included and like we belong. What a small effort on our part to create big value for our kids.

What are the areas of your home and physical surroundings that you could change up with a kid's help? Are you comfortable with the idea of sharing that creative process with them? What boundaries do you need as an adult to make that a fun and engaging experience?

Clear Communication

So many conflicts are born of miscommunication. Communication is fucking complicated. Have you thought about what it means to have a conversation with another person? Your brain creates a series of electrical impulses and thinks of a thing to say, and it sends that thing through a series of filters (your experiences). Then, you say it out loud to another person who hears it, and their brain converts it into a series of electrical impulses, and then proceeds to take it through their own unique filters and wow. How do we ever communicate effectively with other humans? It's pretty impressive that we have any interactions without miscommunications.

Add to that basic communication exchange the processing it takes to form a thought. In milliseconds, your brain can catalogue thousands of memories and experiences and come up with a takeaway message to share with someone else. That processing is internal, invisible, and quick. That's why sometimes Bonnie has whole conversations with herself in her head before coming to a conclusion, which is the part she says out loud. So here she is, driving along and thinking some big thing, but the only part that is said out loud is something like "Oh, of course it was the turtle all along," and all the other people in the car are like "What the fuck are you talking about?" because they weren't privy to all the processing that came before, making that statement seem out of context. Obviously she's talking about some key takeaway from a trip to the zoo, keep up people!

So, how does that understanding of processing and communication play into your parenting interactions? Well, that's all fertile ground for miscommunication and hurt feelings. To avoid that, we have to take some of that processing from being solely internal and turn it into something we say out loud so others understand how we got to the punch line.

Take a deep breath before talking with your kids. Use "I statements" like "I like when dirty socks are put away in the hamper and not left on the floor. When I see dirty socks on the floor, I feel frustrated and annoyed. What I need is for everyone to pick up their own socks and put them in the hamper." Statements like this say exactly what you mean, feel, and need. When giving instructions, focus on one piece at a time. Kids are learning to operationalize tasks that you take for granted, like how a person needs both socks and shoes to go play outside. Kids need stepwise instructions for stuff like that. "First, you need socks, okay? Tell me when you've got some ready." Cut your communication into smaller, more manageable chunks to help set everyone up for success.

Help your kids find the right words, too. When her toddler was in full freak-the-hell-out mode, Bonnie would say "I hear you feeling really overwhelmed now. Take a break and we will talk when you're ready to use your words." Stay close by, so they know you're not abandoning the big feelings in the room, and then let them regroup and try again. Self-regulation is an important part of clear communication and involves being able to control your big feelings enough that you can use your voice. It's a skill we have to learn from others.

This type of clear communication is necessary for one of the key pieces of parenting, which is attachment. Attachment is a deep and real connection we feel with another person; it's a relationship of safety, security, and reliability. Attachment requires empathy, compassion, honesty, and vulnerability. Secure attachment helps people manage tough experiences and loss with more resilience. It's built, like trust, with small, frequent actions. Think of it like a quilt you're making together with your kids. Each stitch, each square, makes the quilt stronger, bigger, and more comfy. Those stitches are made from compassion, clear communication, integrity, and with real and deep love. Your quilt keeps your kids (and you) feeling secure and cozy even when storms are knocking around the windows. Your quilt is made from quality materials and can travel with your kids to any place they choose to go. They can choose people to add to their quilt party, too. Over time, the quilt becomes even softer and warmer; it's a touchstone of your lives together.

If clear communication helps you stitch the quilt, unclear communication puts holes in it. Harsh, aggressive, or thoughtless communication makes your quilt less warm and durable. It's not completely avoidable to have some holes; everyone has a missed stitch sometimes. But clear communication can be used to patch up and repair those holes. Attachment thrives between people when there are early and effective repair attempts when something goes wrong. Effective repair reflects how well we can come back together after a freakout; clear communication makes these attempts more successful, more often.

What does effective repair look like? Some common components of repair include (1) a chance for everyone to share their feelings, (2) a chance for everyone to feel validated in their experience of the conflict, (3) a chance to identify and share triggers that may have contributed to the conflict, (4) a chance for everyone to take responsibility for their role in the conflict, and (5) time for planning how things can go differently next time.

For example, Bonnie and her daughter recently had a fight while cleaning the kid's room. It started as a small spark and turned quickly into a big fire. They yelled at each other and then retreated to different rooms to cool off; they both felt disoriented by how quickly the exchange had escalated. When they came back together, Bonnie said something like "I feel sad that we got angry so quickly about something small. I think you felt frustrated that I was telling you how to make the bed and you were ignoring my suggestions. That's a trigger for me because I really don't like to feel ignored. I wish I had asked for a break before I started yelling at you and if this happens again, I will ask for a break."

Repair is so important because something like a fight about making the bed is not worth leaving a rip in your quilt. You want that quilt to get warmer and softer, not threadbare and holey. Show respect to your kids and the relationship you're building together by being vulnerable enough to work through the repair process. Attachment thrives when there's room for mistakes to be both made and repaired.

People who are deeply connected and attached to one another will not fight to win. They will fight to understand each other better. When you're in conflict with your loved ones, can you take that approach?

What are some ways you and your kids are making your quilt? Are there holes that need your attention? How can you make your quilt bigger and more comfortable? What changes to your communication approach are you willing to make? What will your repair language sound like?

Love Languages

Gary Chapman's book *The 5 Love Languages* is one of those huge bestsellers with a zillion spin-offs, at a level that our little, writerly asses can't even fathom. And for good reason . . . it's a really good model for looking at how we communicate love. Love isn't a feeling, after all. It's a behavior.

Now the book is heteronormative, gendernormative, and Judeo-Christian, with scripture quotes. Not at the level of Jerry Falwell, ("It's Hate and Bake, and I helped!") thankfully. But we say that with the caveat that we know most of us don't fit neatly in all (if any) of those categories. Faith admits that she's totally hacked his love language quiz when using it in groups to be more inclusive. If you decide to take the quiz, you may have to do the same thing in your mind.

But, anyway, digression. The point is we all have ways that we express love and wish to receive love. Chapman refers to these categories as: Acts of Service, Quality Time, Touch, Words of Affirmation, and Gifts. Faith loved discussing these categories with her kiddos (both bio and bonus kiddos—a term she borrowed from Jada Pinkett Smith—otherwise known as her nonrelated niblings). They loved being asked about their love language. And it helped us shape our parenting in relationship to them.

Now Faith's son (Kid #2) say Gifts is his love language. And the dude likes getting shit. Which is all good. But his real love language? Words of affirmation. He thrives on praise. And needs to be praised for something more than once to reinforce it for him. And it's really important to remember that when she's all "Buddhadamn, I'm busy child . . . go away." But praising him fills his love cup and helps reinforce his positive behaviors. Win-win.

Most people take the Love Language quiz and say "What the fuck? I don't want to have to choose just one of these!" You're not choosing just one. You're focusing in on the one that lands the deepest for you so you can clearly communicate that experience to others. And it gives you a way to ask others about their experience and what lands most deeply for them. It's a beautiful and positive way to build a relationship because you get to say to someone, "I will love you in all these ways, but which way will hit you the hardest?" and then be able to give them a big warm fuzzy feeling of validation and acceptance. That's some good emotional shit right there.

Therapeutic Manipulation Techniques

Faith and Bonnie are about to give you something they spent many hours and student loan dollars in mastering: therapeutic manipulation. "What?" you say. "Manipulation is bad and something that hurts people!" And to that we say "Yeah, most of the time. But not this time!"

Because therapeutic manipulation is simply a way to decrease resistance against doing the right thing. It's not manipulating people into things *you* think they should do, or things that might hurt them, or things that protect your own ego and interests. It's a way to get people to do the thing that is right *for them* by attaching it to their own value system and approaching it as if it's a done deal. Like:

- "You are so much smarter than I was about these kinds of things at your age. I know that I don't even need to tell you that you should . . ."

- "Some people would just . . ., but I know you don't roll like that and are going to handle it by doing . . . or . . ."

- "Did you notice they handled that in a way that was pretty selfish? Like doing . . .? I'm so glad you don't act like that!"

Therapeutic manipulation is meant to be thoughtful and empathetic, because it requires knowing someone pretty well to use it effectively. You have to know a person's value system and what they are likely to do in situations in which their values are called upon. You have to use it sparingly because "With great power comes great responsibility, Peter Parker Parent."

This is Parenting Tai Chi, y'all. And one of Faith's clients just recently told her, "I loved how you totally got me to do the right thing without once telling me what to do or how shitty I was for not wanting to do it right off the bat." So even when we know what's happening, we still respond well to that kind of dialogue.

Faith does this all the time with her clients (and for those of you reading this now and thinking, *"heyyy???"* Yup, totally did it. It worked though, right?).

Work to See Your Kids the Way Other People Do

We know you love your kid. Bonnie will admit she's straight-up obsessed with her kid. But we spend a lot of time with those kids and they don't always bring their A game. They are grouchy, and hangry, and they talk back and leave their shoes on the stairs even though we've told them 60 bazillion times not to do that. And because our brains pay a lot more attention to negative stuff (thanks, negativity bias) it's easy to start to feel that negative energy seeping into your interactions. So it can feel jarring at times when you go to parent-teacher conference and the teacher is like "OMG your kid is such a joy to have in class! They are helpful and respectful and they never make a mess!" and you're in your head like *But that little asshole just spilled red Kool-Aid all over my backseat!!* It's jarring because it brings up complicated emotions for us as parents. We want to feel the swell of pride we get when we hear things like that about our kids. We want to believe we are raising exactly that kid who is helpful and kind and thoughtful about shared spaces. And we may also feel a little envious that the teacher gets these interactions and we rarely do. Or we may feel confused about how our experiences can be so different. We get wrapped up in the day-to-day stressors and we forget all the things that make them great. Seeing their good qualities through fresh eyes helps decrease overwhelming feelings, discontent, resentment, and helps us see our parental successes. It's a good reminder about how your hard work is paying off, even when it doesn't seem like it.

And! Often, your kid puts on their best behavior for other people, right? So when you look through someone else's eyes, you're seeing the topflight abilities of this kid you're in the trenches with at home. It's a refreshing perspective and an excellent reminder that you're raising a kid you *want* to see interacting in the world. You can use the knowledge of their best abilities as fuel for your clear communication and focused, authentic praise. Reassure yourself that your kid shows you their toughest behavior because they trust you to handle it maturely and safely; they feel secure enough to act like turds. You can hold both of those extremes for them because all of those pieces are true. Our kids are turds, and they are star students, and they are expert mess-makers, and they do trust us to give them space for all of those experiences. Your job is to make space in your mind for the ways other people see your kids' strengths and assets.

Validate the Choices Your Kids Make and Help Them Learn from Mistakes

Sometimes, our kids choose things we wouldn't have chosen or maybe think isn't a great idea. And then they do it anyway and it turns out great! And our human impulse is to be all *well, look at you; everyone gets lucky sometimes,* in a bitter voice. But try this instead: "I wouldn't have picked that for you," or "I didn't think that would have worked, but you did a great job; it looks great!" because this says to your kid: *Look at you! You knew yourself, you made a good choice based on that knowledge, and you were more right about this than the powerful people in your life!*

That can be a hard one, because we've known our kids for a long time. We've guided them and watched them grow. We've supported them based on what we thought was best with the best information we had at the time. So when our kids go rogue . . .

whew. That's a tough space because we've made it this far on the fuel of our own adult assuredness. But we've also been modeling that assuredness for our kids, and they need to know that they can trust their instincts, too.

Real talk: sometimes those choices are bad as hell, or even dangerous or problematic, or maybe the choice wasn't bad but it still didn't work out for them. How can we validate those choices for our kids using this model? Remember that all of our failures are training grounds. Use those chances to say to your kid "I wouldn't have picked that for you for many reasons. You tried anyway and maybe you don't feel great about the outcomes. What have you learned about yourself from this experience? What do you want to try differently next time? What were some of the factors that guided you toward this decision?" These types of conversations require empathy and compassion; your tired, frazzled parental heart is big enough to hold those feelings along with anger or worry about the situation. Approaching with compassion can help everyone process shame in a way that is constructive instead of entrenching.

Sometimes their decisions have serious consequences and they will need your support to manage the outcomes. You still want to aim to validate the process they used to make the decision and help them identify spots they might have made a different move. We all make decisions all the time that have unintended or unforeseen effects. Kids will need your guidance in taking responsibility for their role and for the ways they can contribute to repair of damaged property or relationships.

A reminder too about brain development. The parts of our brains associated with planning ahead and imagining consequences don't come fully online until around the age of 25. There's somewhat limited brain ability to complete some of these cognitive tasks and even the most mature young person needs additional adult guidance through decision-making processes. Just because they look grown and talk grown doesn't mean they don't need your input, so stay involved and inquisitive in their decisions.

Turns out, both parents and kids are humans. And humans fuck up. Like, a lot. Mistakes and failures are the chances we are given to grow, if, that is, we take time to acknowledge and learn from those mistakes. This means we are straightforward and honest about the ways we've messed up. It means we don't try to hide, deny, or cover up behaviors that are hurtful. It means we say to someone supportive, "This happened and I feel like shit about it. Can you [help me, forgive me, guide me, love me anyway]?" If we as adults take this approach, it will become the default for our kids. What a beautiful way to build resilience, kindness, and humility that also builds trust and strength in your parent-offspring relationship.

Mistakes are chances to repair, to mend, to make your relationships stronger. But to make a mistake can feel icky. To acknowledge that mistake, to yourself or others, can take a lot of courage. Shame makes us tempted to cover up or ignore a mistake in the hopes that no one else will see our misstep. Your job is to take a deep breath, acknowledge any defensiveness you feel, and turn your compassion on full blast. Your ability to show emotional vulnerability will make your relationships more elastic and resilient overall.

Perfection is something people believe they want, but really, perfection is boring. "Perfection" is a white-lady Instagram influencer doing a tree pose in front of a sunset, a snapshot that omits the subsequent loss of equilibrium and the ungainly squawk that burbled from her throat. It's not interesting, it doesn't challenge anyone, and it's an incomplete picture. Think of the people in your life you love to spend time with the most. We would wager they are far from perfect; they are awkward and vulnerable and bad at parallel parking. They bring challenges and mistakes and they are interesting! Bonnie works with a lot of clients who have anxiety and it's often rooted in perfectionism and the shame that comes with mistakes. During one session, a client was processing some of these feelings and said "I think maybe perfect is like uncooked flour. It looks unblemished but no one wants to eat it." Is that not the coolest simile ever?

Give Feedback like a Pro

A lot of clients come to therapy with that goal of managing perfectionism or they have a lot of anxiety around taking feedback or criticism. Many of us, when we were kids, were not approached with empathy when it came time for feedback, and we formed protective coping skills to avoid those interactions because they felt icky. We either strived for perfection so we could be above criticism, or we became good at hiding mistakes so we could avoid criticism. Those behaviors were important to help us feel safer, but as adults, it's limiting to be fearful of feedback. We have to do a lot of emotional work to untangle our fear and shame responses from those childhood experiences. As we begin to parent our own kids, we want them to have a different experience of feedback and critique. When Faith was training to be a board supervisor, her professor taught the class to give feedback in the following format: positive, positive, negative, positive. And if it works with grown-ass people with graduate degrees, maybe kids could benefit from not being negged out all the time, as well, eh?

The idea is simple. Kiddo is sent to clean their room. When you go to check on them, you see they have maybe not done the very best job, even though they know your expectations and you told them how to do it. You might want to get sarcastic or snarky, but let's try this feedback approach: "You did a great job getting all the laundry put away, and I like how you organize all the books on your desk, I bet that will make getting homework done easier! The floor still needs to be swept, but the clean sheets on your bed look great, so I think you're nearly done!"

This works far, far, better than saying, "Did you lose the fucking broom?" And your kid is all "No, I just couldn't get to it cuz you have it stuck up your ass again!" Aaand now all peace treaties are off.

Yeah, it can be a pain in the ass. Especially when you have to be creative in finding the positives. But Faith swears it has cancelled out so many potential arguments at Casa Harper Verde, it's well worth the expenditure of emotional energy!

We all have scripts we use for interactions like this. What are your scripts and where did they come from? Are you a recovering perfectionist who struggles with feedback? Are you too critical of your kids' attempts at new things or giving feedback that lands harshly? Or are you avoiding giving feedback altogether because of your own experiences with it? Are you giving feedback in a way that can be heard and integrated, or do people around you shut down when you try to share these ideas with them? Are you building your relationship by offering growth areas compassionately? If your scripts aren't serving your family relationships, it's time for a rewrite.

Create a Family Team

Aim for as equal distribution as possible in things like chores, bedtime routines, cooking and cleanup, and all the other necessary tasks you need to complete to keep a house running. If you're partnered, have a real conversation about this with your partner and find a balance that avoids relying on stereotypes or burdens one partner over another. Bonnie knows a couple that spent a whole week writing down the minutes they spent doing chores and then reviewed at the end of the week and redistributed tasks in areas that weren't balanced and fair. Maybe you're not data-driven to that level; that's cool. But take time to examine your processes and commit to balance in the ways that make your family more feminist.

And discuss with your children that the tasks are divided in a way that makes the most sense for your family. Maybe one adult stays home so they do more of the work around the house. Maybe Mom cooks because she *likes* cooking, not because that's what women do. Talk about how those roles are decided and why, rather than presume they understand. Otherwise, the gender norms in media will raise a false flag for them.

Every night at bedtime, Bonnie tells her daughter a few things she appreciates about her. The constants are about her kindness, curiosity, and loving spirit; the rest of the list is particular to the day. Giving specific compliments like, "I really appreciate how you picked up the trash you found in the yard today. It shows you care about our home and the environment," help your child recognize the ways they contribute to your family and home. And it's a lovely and peaceful way to wrap up your day.

Spend some time talking with your kids about all the ways a family can look and function. Emphasize the ways in which everyone in your family works together for the health and happiness of the group. List the ways that you care for and about each other, and think of ways you can show appreciation for that. Talk about different family structures that your family or their friends' families could take on: hetero parents, same-sex parents, single parents, grandparents-as-parents, stay-at-home parents, adoptive/foster parents, and the ways we can create families out of our friends.

Think of the language that you want to model, and negotiate it as needed. Faith uses the term "bonus children" to describe the kids in her life that she considers family, because the term "stepchildren" and other terms felt icky. She will cheerfully say she has thirteen kids. When people look askance, she responds with "I only actually gave birth to a couple of them . . . . . .but they're all mine!" She also respects how her kids relate to each other ("That's my brother" or "That's my cousin") . . . because it's about the emotional content of the relationship, not the biological family tree structure.

Choose a Family Motto, Guide Word, or Value

Your family is a team. Your team is unique. There is no other family like your family. Isn't that fantastic? That's something to celebrate and make a big deal of. That's something that deserves a souvenir T-shirt! But what will you put on your T-shirt? May we suggest an outrageous family motto?

Sit together with your family and brainstorm some words or values that you appreciate or have meaning to you as a group. Come to a consensus on a few words that can guide your family life and decisions out in the world. Bonnie's family value is "kindness" and they chose it together. They can revisit it when they feel lost, confused, or angry. Bonnie can say to her daughter,

"Our family values kindness. Does this action fit our value?" or, "Remember: we agreed to choose kindness." It's a gentle reminder that they have a family goal of doing no harm to each other or others in their lives.

It's great if your motto is easy to remember, maybe a little fun, and acceptable to shout in public as you drop them off at school. Some additional Scott family faves include, "Don't talk about it, be about it!" and, "Be a problem solver, not a problem maker!" Because they are that kind of obnoxious family. Your family mottos are yours and can be as obnoxious and/or meaningful as you want.

What are the values that bring you together as a family? What ideals guide your decisions and activities? How do you keep those principles at the forefront of your mind? Will they fit on your souvenir T-shirt?

Conclusion

Well, there you have it: our list of guiding principles to open conversations about how you want your family to be and the ways you want your kids to be in the world. The ideas can be summed up as: "Be kind, be compassionate, be responsible, be supportive," because your goal is to create a space where your kids feel included and understood. We hope it's a list that serves you in searching yourself and your family for the places you can be more empathic and more imperfect. We also hope that you'll honor the gift you've been given by regularly reminding yourself (out loud, a note on your mirror, a pop-up calendar reminder) that even when parenting is hard af, it's an honor bestowed on us by the universe. That we have been paired with these people, to guide and love them, is no accident, and this deserves respect. We have to remember that we can hold conflicting ideas without our heads popping off our necks . . . we will enjoy our kids *and* be the person responsible for setting them straight in the world.

Part of the privilege of parenting is the fact that it is hard as *fuck*. Worthwhile work is rarely easy or able to be done on autopilot. Parenting requires presence, vulnerability, empathy, and patience. Those abilities are hard because they are worth the work. Parenting is one of those chances to human at your highest levels. The invitation to offer your best self to the process of forming new psyches; that's some deep emotional stuff right there.

Fun fact. Two out of two authors of this book recognize that this section was a lot, in and of itself. And freely admit they are works-in-progress in this area. Zero percent of anything in this book is designed to "out-woke" you and make you feel like a parenting failure. We already have social media to do that. It is about the journeys that all of us are on so we can remember our prime direction (nerd joke!) as humans responsible for the care and feeding of other humans. But that aside? Shall we take a break from some of that deep emotional stuff? Okay, yeah, we are feeling that emotional hangover too. Let's jump now into some more specific skills and processes your kids and family will need as you navigate the world you're building together.

NAVIGATING WHO WE ARE AND INTERSECTIONAL ISSUES OF SOCIAL JUSTICE

One of Faith's teen clients recently told her that Gen Z is just waiting for the neocon olds to die off so they can change the world. And we are both pretty sure they will. The people who think they can change the world are generally the ones that do. But we also know it's a tall order, and we need to support and encourage their growth and empathy and humanity so they can do so. How can you learn, be open, and help kids navigate some of the toughest topics we face as a society? What are some ways to widen the safe space you've created in your home into the community and institutions your kids will encounter as they move through life? How can you manage your own traumas and fears in ways that are helpful to you while simultaneously guiding a younger person through the process of processing?

Race

When Faith's older kid was about eight years old, Faith was driving home and they saw a woman getting arrested in a nearby neighborhood. The police were frisking her and cuffing her against the police car as we were driving by.

Her kid said, "What are they doing?"

Faith responded, "Well, it looks like she's getting arrested."

Her kid was confused, "But she's white, and only Black people get arrested!"

It turns out that Faith's kid had been watching *Law & Order* with grandma and was being flooded with all the stereotypical images of what criminals look like. It was a *huge* wake-up call that these kinds of issues needed to be discussed proactively and repeatedly. She couldn't just model the values that were important to her and hope for the best. She had to be fighting *for* her kids *against* the larger culture.

Race is a topic that is all-encompassing to American life. It always has been, but for modern parents, it has been even more front and center over the past decade. The protests in the summer of 2020 were another very visible example of the need to proactively discuss race in our homes and to actively make changes in our relationships and communities.

In the summer of 2020, Bonnie's daughter was six. She saw the protests on TV and started asking questions about what she saw. Bonnie's had a lot of tough conversations with her kid over the years, but talking about the police brutality of 2020 was something else altogether. Bonnie and her kid both felt the gravity and urgency of the conversation, but Bonnie moved through it as slowly and thoughtfully as she could. The conversation that specific day ended with them talking about the parents of the people who were killed that summer and how much they must miss their kids who were taken too soon. And then they checked out some books about the history of civil rights and they made donations to social justice organizations in their community. The conversation is important, but it isn't enough. We can show our kids that we learn, we grow, and then we show up, in all the ways we can, to do the work. And we continue to engage with these tough topics. One conversation and a few well-meaning donations don't get the job done or let us off the hook, but we also can't pass up chances to do those things.

These conversations mean we have to wrestle with some shame. Shame of our privilege, or our lack of knowledge / understanding of history, or that we are descendants of people who were involved in the institution of slavery. We are not the decisions our ancestors made; we can choose to be accountable to the history of slavery and systemic racisim by actively working against it. Even if your family owned a plantation—you can choose love and activism, and you can own the fact that slavery was monsterous. We haven't met anyone demanding that people apologize for the actions of their ancestors, but what we are demanding is necessary societal change. The legacy of slavery lives in white supremacy; how do your actions push back against or perpetuate this system of violence?

Families of color in the United States have necessary conversations about race very early in the lives of their children; studies show that white families do not do the same. White families report that they feel the need to wait for some "safe" or "right" time to talk to their kids about race and racism. And colorism. Faith and her kids are mixed, but have enough pass privilege to have a different experience of the world than someone more melanated. The right time to talk about racism is immediately. And repeatedly. Race relations in the U.S. are fraught and raw, and having real discussions and action is more imperative than ever. We can't shield our children with this *"I don't see color"* bullshit. I mean, as of this writing you can in Texas, where teaching children about structural racism in the classroom is now illegal. But let's not, ok? The work of dismantling racism belongs to all of us, of course, but white families must own more of the work than they have in the past. To be silent, to stand aside, to decline to participate—it is unacceptable. The time for action is now, and your feminist family is the place to start.

The general discussions you're engaging in with your family, about power and safety and allyship, lead many families into discussions specifically about race and systemic racial inequalities.

Don't think it's done or they get it. We never know when a *Law &*
Order–esque counter message has infiltrated their subconscious
and is informing their view of the world.

As parents, we know that each time we tell our child goodbye at
school drop-off or as they walk out the front door with friends,
it could be the last time. None of us are guaranteed safety in
this life, and understanding mortality is among the higher-stress
truths of parenthood. But, if you are the parent of a white (or
"passing") child, understand that your child will be given the
benefit of the doubt in situations that children of color will not.
Your white child is less likely to be harassed or killed by police, is
less likely to be arrested for a minor crime, and is more likely to
come home to you safely. Understand this, and then dive into the
work that needs to be done to help all our kids be safer.

One of the ongoing effects of white supremacy is colorism and
passing. People with lighter skin are often viewed more favorably
than people with darker skin, and that's just straight-up systemic
racism showing up in another place in our lives. Faith has one side
of the family that showed some distinct colorism bullshit recently.
One of the assorted kiddos is much darker than the rest, even
though most are multiracial. And some racist/colorist bullshit
ensued, which became yet another fucking growth opportunity
within the entire family about the issue. And praise be to every
momma bear involved for being loud and insistent that this wasn't
an "apologize and move on" situation.

Bonnie has been doing some deep emotional work recently
with several clients who are coming to terms with the effects of
colorism in their own families. They've seen and experienced that
other family members get better treatment if they have lighter
skin, and that's hurtful. Because white supremacy operates in

a hierarchy of power (where the power comes from being pale af), all the degrees of whiteness/paleness come with degrees of power within the system. It really sucks to see that play out in our own experiences and within our own families where we want to be loved and accepted wholly. What are your experiences with white supremacy and colorism in your family or life? Are you carrying any of those internalized biases that may be affecting you or your family?

Bonnie has a friend who is the mom of two teenage boys who are Black. They are among only a handful of Black boys in their peer group. Bonnie's friend talks to them all the time about how they don't have the leeway of doing normal stupid teenager shit, because they will not be afforded the "stupidity of youth" defense. They could be shot and killed for ding-dong-ditching the wrong house because of their skin color, whereas white or lighter-skinned teen boys might make it out with a stiff talking-to. These are the realities of parents around us, and parents have to stick together. White families need to have tough conversations, do it early, and keep it going so that we can raise a new generation of white kids who can carry on our anti-racism work. It is imperative.

Doing anti-racism work is far from easy. It can take a real toll on your mental and spiritual health. Building up your self-care routine, and showing this to your kids, is an important part of keeping up the pace. So often, we feel real physical pain when we read the news or engage in racial work; we have to take time to replenish and come back to the work with newfound tenacity every single time.

Obviously, this could be a whole book in and of itself. This book is an overview of a lot of different shit, not an in-depth analysis of anything in particular. So with this topic, *especially* this topic, please seek out writing and ideas from people of color. Look for workshops and gatherings in your area that center on race and racism. Do the work of unpacking white privilege yourself with other activists and scholars. Look for and fight against racism in the institutions that have shaped your life. Share the background and additional information you learn with your children. Encourage your children to talk about their experiences with race and racism and help them navigate this complicated landscape with empathy and courage.

Gender

Ah, gender. What a fantastic part of human life. The ways it defines us, our relationships, our interactions with the world . . . gender, as a construct, is powerful. So, let's talk about it, shall we?

How do you define gender? What messages have you gotten about gender, gender expression, or gender roles, and how does this play out in your life?

Gender is a range of characteristics and felt senses that may include relation to biological sex, sex-based social structures, or gender identity/expression. It's the way we experience life along the spectrum of "maleness" to "femaleness," and these experiences are diverse and impacted by many factors, including our culture, our religion, our family of origin, and our own feelings about our gender.

How do you define and experience your own gender? How do you communicate that definition to other people in your life? How do you express your felt sense of gender in various areas of life?

Gender exists along a continuum of experiences and can be very fluid for some people and very rigid for others. This may vary based on age, where someone lives, and the overall culture a person lives within.

Kids get a lot of messages about gender and gender roles. Just look at toy aisles in a store; the message is clear that cars and swords are "boy toys" and dolls and kitchens are "girl toys." That is shifting somewhat, but kids are definitely soaking up some traditional/stereotypical gender messages. So you may see your own kid leaning hard into those stereotypical roles because they feel comfortable there. You may also see your kids lean hard into the "opposite" role to see how that feels for them. These are normal explorations of gender expression and it's cool to see more and more parents embrace these experiences. Just as adults experience gender differently at different times in our lives or different spheres, kids experience this fluidity as well. As they grow, you may notice them experimenting with the ways they express gender (think clothing, hairstyles, name, or pronouns) and that can be sort of jarring for some parents. In her office, Bonnie coaches parents to relax when they are concerned about this; hairstyles and pronouns aren't permanent, so it's okay for kids to play around with them. No harm done.

Most kids will experiment with gender presentation and try on different personas during their lifetimes. This is a pretty typical part of development. For some kids, though, it may seem like it's more than an experiment. If your child is consistent, persistent, and insistent that they are a different gender than the one assigned to them at birth, it may be more than exploration. As more visibility and support are accessible for people in the trans community, it's becoming more common for young people to identify openly as trans. Support your child by being open and listening to their feelings. Many trans and gender non-conforming (GNC) adults can tell you about how they knew their truths very early in their lives, but not everyone knows from a young age, so this may happen at any time—even after they've moved out and are on their own. A safe and affirming home and school experience is invaluable as people are defining their gender experiences.

Supporting your child early is one important way to help them navigate their gender. A good starting point is to find support for yourself in an online community like PFLAG or your local LGBTQ groups. Most larger communities have peer-led groups and family outing activities you can check out. We live in the deep and scary South but have both served on (different!) boards that provide these types of services. Additionally, there may be resources at your child's school; lots of schools have gay-straight alliance groups (GSAs) that work to create inclusive school spaces. Leverage the resources around you and see where there may be holes in the support network.

You may want to create a team of gender-affirming professionals to support your family in the process. Bonnie has a lot of trans teens on her caseload, and therapy sessions are generally spent talking about hopes, fears, challenges, and questions about what it means to be trans or deciding to transition either socially or medically, along with the general stressors that all teens face, regardless of gender expression. She also has several parents of teens who are trans. Those sessions give space to parents who are scared their child may be discriminated against or be otherwise unsafe, for questions about the transition process, and even processing the grief that accompanies big changes in life. Your family deserves support and an affirming space to process the big feelings that come with shifting identities.

Families of trans kids face specific types of stressors. They have to be ready to advocate for safe spaces in school (getting teachers and administrators to use correct pronouns and names, allowing kids to use the restroom of their gender, or managing bullying). There may be transphobia within the family's social circle or extended family members (like grandparents, family friends, or church). Recently, conservative state legislatures have targeted trans youth with nasty bills that limit their ability to seek gender-affirming care, that prohibit trans youth from participating in sports, or enforce bathroom/locker room use to "birth gender." These examples of systemic transphobia can be devastating to trans youth and their families, and are a unique stressor in their daily lives. If your child is trans, you're going to need a strong support system to help you manage the discrimination and aggressions your family may face.

At the same time, Bonnie has a few clients who come from families who are not affirming, supportive, or interested in their gender. If your child is trans and you find you're struggling to engage on the topic, please at least find them a safe adult they can talk about it with. Trans youth whose families are not affirming are much more likely to die by suicide than other teens. Gender is powerful in our lives, and if parents cannot affirm and support trans kids, the rejection is felt deeply. You will have your own feelings about your child's gender, and that's valid, but please connect them to a safe adult while you process on your own.

Okay, so, how do you want to start to talk about gender in your family? How do you see gender expression happening for your child or their friends? You might have practice, "What if

. . . " conversations, like, "What if your friend tells you they are trans? Like, he's spending the night at the house, and y'all are playing video games, and he says, 'Oh by the way, I was born with a vagina'?" Let them think out loud about the ways they can support their friends. What is their own experience of gender and what do they see in their social groups or classes? What do they want to know and what do they need to know? What might make their friend feel comfortable versus uncomfortable in the process? Help them troubleshoot problematic relationships and show that you support them in forming their own ideas and approaches. Help them recognize and remove themselves from toxic people and situations.

Basic rule here, alright? There are no "boy things" or "girl things," okay?

There are just "toys" or "clothes" or whatever. Boys can like what they want. Girls can like what they want. People can like what they want. That rule will help you with so many gender ideas and questions. It gives you permission to give kids of all ages the space to experiment with gender. To have freedom to find the activities, toys, clothes, and *lives* that spark their interests and give them joy. Get your gendered ideas about stuff out of here right now, and start by being aware of the moment when all the messages that you grew up with start sprouting up like weeds in your conversations.

Adults have hang-ups about gender. Kids don't, until we force our hang-ups onto them. So own your hang-ups and don't force them onto your kids. If this idea is uncomfortable for you, start small. Be more flexible with the gender of characters in books or movies. If gender isn't explicit, leave it open with a "they" (a totally acceptable gender-neutral pronoun), or try mixing it up.

Occasionally, Bonnie's daughter will ask "Is that a boy or a girl?" about a character in a book or movie. Bonnie always answers with "What do you think?" and her daughter will say something like "I don't know; maybe it's just a cow?" Like, on further inspection, maybe it doesn't matter.

Maybe the Shy Little Kitten is a girl when you read the story on Tuesday and a boy when you read it on Wednesday. Point out astronauts that are women and men that are teachers. Lean into your discomfort with ambiguous or flexible gender and see how it feels to be more open. Let that flexibility guide you into bigger areas, like toys, clothes, and careers. Don't limit your kid's imagination or potential by creating boxes full of gendered stuff and then forcing your kid into those boxes.

If your kids have questions about gender and gender non-conforming behavior, talk about how that's changed over time. Show them old pictures online, and point out that women used to always wear dresses because that's what they were supposed to do. And now we know how silly that is, because sometimes women wear jeans because they like them better and think they're more comfortable. And sometimes boys wear dresses, because they like them better and think they're more comfortable.

And there are all kinds of ways gender can present. While Faith's son is pretty cishet manly (he's pretty much an epic bro, and Bonnie can attest to that), he does like to experiment with scents, and will sometimes wear her perfume with his suit and tie. He finds it hilarious when women ask him "Dude . . . is that Chanel No. 5?"

Combatting the cultural marketing of gender roles (otherwise known as "Help! A Disney princess ate my kiddo's brain!")

Parents of younger kids probably recognize the princess-centered obsession that starts around the same time your kid might be questioning gender. Princessdom is ubiquitous because animated movie songs are catchy as hell and being a princess seems like a pretty glam job. We get it. Our advice is: don't panic about princesses! Your kid will likely be obsessed for a while because their friends are obsessed. You can take time to talk with your kid about how being a princess is a job, and that some people do it and in a way that is public service oriented and important, but it's not a job most people will be able to achieve.

The role model aspects of fictional princesses have changed and grown over the years, thank Buddha. Now we can talk about how Anna and Elsa saved each other. Mulan kicks some serious butt, and she can be an inspiration for all children interested in martial arts. Moana (not technically a princess) is a *boss*; she's physically and emotionally intelligent, while maintaining her sense of fun. And what about General Leia? The one member of the Skywalker/Organa clan who never wavered in her belief in the Force even when all the guys around her did, and who spent her whole life in public service and diplomacy.

Even the old-school Disney ladies have good qualities we can focus on. Asking questions like "How can you take care of animals like Snow White?" can be a great starting point (or even pointing out that she has to clean up after a bunch of damn dwarves when your kiddo only has to put their toys back in the bin!). "It looks like Princess Jasmine is a good advocate; she stands up for herself and her family even when it's hard. What are some jobs people do that involve advocacy and standing up for people?" Questions and conversations like these can be helpful to your kid in separating fantasy from reality.

When Bonnie's kid is in her princess phase and wants to read fairy tales for days, we change the endings to be more fun. Like Prince Charming and Princess Aurora going out for vermicelli bowls so they can get to know each other as friends instead of getting married like, 10 minutes after she wakes up. Or Cinderella feeling such a boost of confidence from her beautiful ball gown that she tells her stepmom to get bent and moves into her own apartment in the city, where she gets a job at Sephora and rescues a cat from the animal shelter.

Sexuality

Sexuality is a different conversation than gender, though they often happen together or in related ways. Gender is how we feel about and express our male/female/nonbinary-ness; sexuality is who we are (or aren't) attracted to romantically or sexually. Just like gender, though, sexuality is a spectrum and can vary over the course of a lifetime. We've already mentioned some general approaches to conversations around this, but we think one key piece of advice is to avoid making assumptions about who our kids may or may not be attracted to later in life. Don't make assumptions that they want to get married at all, or that they will marry or date people of "opposite" sex or gender. A lot of Bonnie's clients are adolescents, and almost all of them have a story about one of their parents saying something like "I don't really care who you date as long as they aren't jerks," and Bonnie really likes this approach. The important parts of dating, sex, and sexuality are the ways we find safety, challenges, and excitement in other people. Encouraging young people in your life to look for the safe and fun people is the key takeaway.

Some people aren't sexually attracted to other people at all. They may or may not enjoy romantic relationships, both of which are also valid ways of being human. It's important to share that a person isn't broken if their sexual and/or romantic orientation is, (D) none of the above, because they may not hear or see that from anyone else.

Our kids will need support in feeling safe to explore their sexuality and sexual/romantic identities. They need to know that if they are LGBTQ, they have adults in their lives who will hold a safe space for letting them figure out how that fits into their overall identity and approach to the world. If they use labels or terminology you're unfamiliar with, please feel free to gently ask what those terms mean to the young person you're talking to. Bonnie has a client who ended up making a PowerPoint presentation when they wanted to come out to their parents as pansexual. They were pretty sure their parents wouldn't know the terminology and they didn't want the conversation to get derailed by definitions. Keep an open mind and open ears; the young person is letting you into a sensitive part of their psyche and identity.

"Coming out" will look different for everyone and is a process, not a singular event. We hope for a day when people don't have to be scared to come out, or maybe they don't have to come out at all, because the world is accepting, there is not a presumed "normal" way to be that we have to announce we don't ascribe to, and people are far less nosy about who we want to love. But for right now, LGBTQ peeps need a safe place to have this conversation, a place where they are affirmed and loved and held as precious. Remember too, that coming out belongs to the person coming out! If they've trusted you, it doesn't mean you go and tell other people about it. Just because they are okay with you knowing doesn't mean they are ready for other people in their life to know; that may even include other parents or family members.

Make sure you're a person who supports LGBTQ youth to come out in their own time, with their own plans, and in the order they choose. And, alternately, if they specifically ask you to tell people, or address issues with other adults that they are facing (you know, misgendering them, telling them that they are just having a "phase," and other crappy behavior) then you absolutely should. This allyship as a verb, right? Giving them authority over how they share their identity, while standing by their side in bodyguard mode is one of the best gifts you can give your kiddo. And it's fuckin' free.

The sexuality conversations you're having with young people in your life will encompass more than coming out, obviously. Being ready to talk about consent, risk-reduction strategies, and other logistics will be helpful. But we think of this conversation more generally as guidance into the sometimes-fraught world of romance, courting, and being respectful of potential partners. The logistics are there, obviously, but this can also be a conversation about all the joy and fun that comes from meeting new people, feeling curious and excited, and learning new things about ourselves by being in these types of relationships.

Religion and Spirituality

This feels like a sticky topic. But we all have some kind of connection with the world outside ourselves. We may express that through religion, spirituality, or some form of secular humanism. And these topics are just as important as any others, even if we don't have some kind of formal religious practice and are not raising our kids with same-said practice.

Faith's parents, while devout Catholics, were also devoutly progressive. There were a lot of conversations about what they loved about the church, what they found challenging, and how their beliefs sat in the discomfort of hoping for change. They also encouraged her to have something bigger than herself. It didn't have to be Catholicism, but it should be something. They encouraged her to attend other churches and discuss what she liked and didn't like. It was pretty amazing to be able to be horrified by a sermon at a friend's church and go home and process that experience with a parent.

And like everything else, we are wanting to give our children a space to grow and to think, right? The way Faith now expresses that "something bigger than oneself" is using the language of Dr. Mary Catherine Bateson. Dr. Bateson was the daughter of Margaret Mead and Gregory Bateson, avowed atheists, while she became Episcopalian. When asked by Nikki Giovanni as part of an interview for the podcast *On Being* about the difference between religion and spirituality, Dr. Bateson's response was, essentially, that we are focusing on the wrong question.

We can express religion or spirituality or some form of secular humanity by rote. Without any real engagement with something bigger. Or we can experience life, in its vast array, with a sense of *wonder*. That is where our sense of purposeful belonging resides. That our belief system, our ritual, our engagement in the process serves to care for people and include them rather than judge and exclude them. As long as that's our operating system, we are aiming for good humaning.

Another piece of this conversation revolves around helping your kid navigate other peoples' religious or spiritual beliefs. Bonnie is not particularly religious, but many people in her life are. She talks to her daughter about how everyone finds their own connection to the world and to other people, and some of us find that in religion. Some of us find it in meditation or volunteering, or any other myriad ways. As long as someone is not using their religious beliefs to oppress another, we can respect each other and be curious about other approaches to the spiritual. Deep and meaningful conversations happen in that curious and mystical space.

Leaving religion and spirituality open to discussion may mean that your kid chooses a really different belief system than the one you possess. How will you handle a kid who is atheist while you're deeply connected to God? What if they are leaning toward a more conservative type of worship system and you're not comfortable with that? Spiritual experiences are deep and personal; it might feel emotionally fraught to have these conversations with your kid when they choose a different path than the one you're on. What space does spirituality or religion hold in your home and is there room for different viewpoints and experiences?

Legal System

How do we discuss something like the legal system? It's flawed and imperfect, but held up as authoritative and definitive. It's based on precedent and bias. It's staffed by a lot of well-meaning people who make honest efforts at protecting people and advocating for victims. It's also full of people who love power and control. Some of the mistakes are incidental; some are baked into the crust. Those errors can be all-encompassing for people in the legal system; they can make it possible to be wrongly convicted, die while incarcerated, or make life very difficult after release.

Obviously, there have to be some rules for a society to function. However, the issue with the American legal system is that white supremacy, gender bias, ableism, and classism all feature too prominently for the system to work for everyone. So, how to talk to kids about something so complicated?

The legal system is integral to our lives and a working knowledge of it is necessary for those of us living within it. Almost everyone will visit a courthouse at some point in our lives. We might go for jury duty, or get married or divorced, or to change our name and gender markers. Some of those life events are really exciting but will still require us to interact with authority figures. We need to understand there's a way to interact with people in those spaces that gets the job done. You may want to discuss your own experiences with courthouses with your kid so they have some idea of how those interactions look. Those interactions require patience and a commitment to asking for guidance; these qualities can be hard for young people to summon if they are under stress.

Extend these conversations to what it looks like to interact with a police officer. Ideally, the interaction is courteous on both sides and everyone walks away safely. Give them the best chance you can for that to happen by coaching them to keep their hands in plain sight, always have their license and insurance with them, explain anything they are doing and reaching for, and to respectfully interact with the authority figure who's just pulled them over. For example, Faith relayed to her kids the story of getting pulled over and telling the officer, "I need to get that out of my glove box, and I know there is an X-Acto knife from a craft project sitting on top of everything, including my insurance card . . . are you okay with me opening my glove box?"

Police pull-overs can be really scary, especially with all of the body cam footage we've collectively watched in recent years. And of course, if that's the part we see, we are well aware of what else is roiling underneath. That's a tough but necessary part of this conversation. There's a guide in the next chapter to help you teach the language we all need to navigate an authoritarian culture. Obviously, authority figures should do better at their jobs so they don't escalate in these ways, but until then, we need to arm our kids with the tools that will give them the best chance of getting out of these interactions safely.

Pop culture and current events can give you an opening to talking about the legal system. Just like Faith's example of her kid watching too much *Law & Order*, messages about interacting with the legal system can be insidious and pervasive. Hold these falsehoods up to the light with your kids around, like "The writers on this show really must think only Black men commit robberies. Every episode I've seen of this show uses that same lazy trope. Have you noticed anything like that?" (Maybe without the expression "lazy trope" unless your kiddo is bougie and also talks like that.)

Politics

Coming into your own capital *P* Political views is a lifelong process and open to many layers of influence. None of us will hold the exact same views as our parents or other role models. We can't expect our kids to have the exact same views as we do. Talking about politics has always been a flashpoint in families; there's a reason there's so many "It's not a family party 'til someone cries," scenes in movies and TV; the majority of us can recognize the scene from our own holiday and birthday tables.

Even in families where people largely agree, the nuance of how we feel about the two-party system, political gridlock, making laws, and the overall role and duty of government varies. With your kids, aim to have conversations that allow for passion, for debate and discourse, but avoid attacking or dismissing. One of the interesting things about politics in general is that it is endlessly debatable; we think the key is making your best effort to keep the table, holiday or otherwise, open for ideas and respectful disagreement. So long as that disagreement is not a matter of treating human beings like human beings versus not treating human beings like human beings. We go back to the same idea we talked about in religion and spirituality. As long as we are centering and imparting a morality that serves to care for people instead of harm them, we're creating a positive foundation for our children. Fiscal responsibility and smaller federal government were the original hallmarks of conservatism, and that's not a bad thing.

Faith and Bonnie both have conservative friends that are even more horrified by actions happening in the name of the political party they had been aligned with than Faith and Bonnie (which says a lot, seeing that we aren't quiet about our progressive politics). Pointing out to our kids that these are people we love and respect is important. We may differ on the idea of the national endowment of the arts, but we all want less violence and more safety for our fellow humans. That's not a budgetary disagreement, that is a fundamental support of humanity.

Democracy, at it's best, is a system that welcomes everyone's input and suggestions. Local politics can sometimes still fit this framework. Bonnie grew up in a very conservative part of Texas, and when she was in fourth grade, she wrote a letter to the mayor detailing her concerns about litter throughout the city along with a few suggestions to help improve the situation. The mayor's office called and she got to go and have a personal meeting with the mayor to talk about it; thus began a lifelong obsession with local politics. In college, she continued the obsession by starting a petition to ask local officials to consider the implementation of a recycling program throughout the city (which was even smaller and more conservative than the place she grew up). The petition did open the door for that conversation and allowed for a pilot program of recycling drop-off stations throughout the city. Local politicians are more likely than state or national officials to still interact in these ways and we hope they will welcome input from kids.

You can take your kids to school board meetings, or city council meetings, or debates during election season. Take them with you to cast your ballot on Election Days; in Texas they get a little "Future Voter" sticker that hopefully will hold true (both because your kid will vote and Texas will fail in suppressing their vote). Our influence is precious and involvement in local politics is a powerful place to exercise it.

Depending on your state, there may be options to be involved in state-level politics as well. You can request meetings with legislators or tour the halls of the legislature. Kids can write letters, make phone calls, or attend protests for issues they feel passionately about. They can get involved with nonprofit advocacy groups to raise money or awareness of topics and issues that are decided in government. Help them tune in for big moments, like Supreme Court nomination hearings or impeachment trials. Government impacts their day-to-day lives in major ways and it's important that they know how it works, how it malfunctions, and how they can be involved.

Part of this process will be preparing your kiddos for how those around them respond to their level of engagement and activism. Prepare your kiddos for society's response to their wokeness. Our country is divided. Not everyone will be down with your kid and their radical attitudes. Teach them to love themselves and trust themselves in the face of doubt, fear, and general shittiness from people who want to tear them down for their badass feminism. Remind them continually about the safe spaces and people in their lives. It's scary out there sometimes; knowing they have someone to call who always has their back is pretty important.

What about the language that helps us navigate an authoritarian culture?

We owe our kids the truth about the importance of using a language of respect when dealing with authority figures, even when those authority figures are awful.

The reality is that there are going to be *many* people in their lives and our lives who have unequal ideas about respect. There will be people in their lives that say, "I'll respect you if you respect me," and what they really mean is, "I will respect your personhood if you respect my authority over your personhood."

And in truth, many of these people will be in positions of power over your children in their lives. And we need our children to be safe in order to survive.

Of course this doesn't mean taking the abuse and bullying lying down. And honestly, protecting our children from all the insidious ways bullying can be present in their lives is likely a far-reaching conversation. But there are a few general guidelines that we all need to keep in mind as parents:

- Tell them not to talk shit to police officers, school authorities, or other individuals in power. Use ma'am or sir. Mr./Ms./Mx./Dr./Rev./Officer/ Sergeant. Whatever the expected markers of respect are in that situation.

- Encourage them not to enter these situations with a chip on their shoulder. While Faith and Bonnie live in Texas and are often embarrassed about the stunts our lawmakers pull, we also live in a large and generally progressive city. Faith was active in training the local police force on respecting language within the trans* and gender nonconforming community. She can attest to how hard many of these officers are really trying to get it right. And they don't have to—they are the ones with the badges and guns. So if they are trying, we can keep trying, too. We need to give each other the benefit of the doubt as much as possible, and not presume an authority figure is intending to be combative.

- If it turns out that someone is violating their rights and their safety, teach your children the skills they need to get out of the situation with minimum impact and damage to themselves and those around them. Follow-up can always happen later.

- Remind them that you are a *safe space*. And teach them who else around them is a safe space. Remind them repeatedly that you will have their back and do everything in your power to protect them. Reiterate that you are not perfect. That you may be distracted and overwhelmed by your own life, so you may not read their nonverbal cues that something is wrong. But you will immediately stop and pay attention if they say, "Something is wrong and I need your help." Remind them that there are other people in their lives who will do the same. Ideally, you will have a point person for your kid in all of their life domains. Their school ally, home ally, neighborhood ally, sports team ally, church ally, etc., etc.

- Teach pragmatic strategies for self-protection. Get your kids enrolled in self-defense courses. Teach them basic activist first aid. Talk to them about filming interactions and show them how to download and use the ACLU app on their phone. Teach them their legal rights (including what information they have to give and what they don't) and how to calmly advocate for those rights if you aren't around—by using calm and polite language with a broken-record discussion technique.

Introducing kids to political action

Bring your kids to marches, political events and town halls, organizing meetings, fundraisers, meetups, and other feminist and anti-racism spaces. In doing this, we show our kids what democracy and resistance look like, and we also advocate for greater inclusion of parents and kids in social justice movements. Many social justice events are organized by young, childless people who don't always think of ways to include our mini-fems. We as parents can work to make every space we inhabit safe enough for our kids to inhabit with us. Bonnie's daughter totally has her own pussy hat, which Bonnie carried in her coat pocket for the whole Women's March on Washington in 2017, and Faith's son has officially spent his entire childhood in community action work. He was the youngest person at the Million Mom March in 2000. He was pushed in a stroller and breastfed at the end.

Bonnie's daughter got to wear that pussy hat to her first march, the International Women's Day march, and carried her own protest sign, which said, at her request, "Happy Women's Day, I love all of you!" That memory is listed among Bonnie's prouder mama moments.

You can also look for events that are designed to be family oriented, not just Angry Protest O'Clock Time. For example, Faith was on the board of the Pride Center San Antonio. We hosted several Pride family events every year and encouraged ally attendance. Kids had a great time, and got to see all the different ways people can comprise a family. Several times, Faiths' son agreed to be the Easter Bunny. Everyone was surprised that he was willing to put on a smelly costume and hug a batrillion kids while getting smeared with chocolate. He shrugged and said, "This is what we do. It's important, and it's fun."

Faith is deeply grateful that's his perspective.

Faith's been feeling overwhelmed as of late, something Bonnie can also deeply relate to. We are all struggling to figure out how much we can do when it feels that we can never do enough. Bonnie and Faith have a mutual friend who is also a community activist, and she and Faith were at a town hall meeting a few years ago protesting a bill that would allow the state to force trans and gender-nonconforming folks to use the bathroom of their birth assignment. At the same time, a few blocks away, a Dreamer youth was being held for deportation by border patrol and there was a protest happening there, as well.

"We need to be there, too," she said, "But we also need to be here. What do we do?"

It feels like there aren't enough of us to be in all the places we need to be to advocate for the world we want. We are online, we are in town halls, we are marching in protests, we are fundraising, and on and on and on, and still it's not enough. And as parents, we weep sometimes. And we want our children to know enough to combat injustice but not overwhelm them or scare them away from seeing all that is good in the world.

Part of carrying discussion into action is talking about the choices we make in action, how and why we make them, and the privilege we have in making them.

How do we find our own peace with these issues and help our children find theirs? Is it a terrible thing to go out to a movie when that money could pay for someone's medication in a developing country? Be honest with your children about everyone's struggles toward finding the middle way.

Find ways to communicate that expressing love in the world means giving the world our work and sacrifice, but also our laughter and joy if we are among the lucky who are allowed that privilege.

If the only world we show our kids is one where everything is awful and there's no fun or joy, what exactly are we fighting for? A world like that doesn't feel worth the effort. But we are fighting for a world where everyone is safer, and more equal, and has more space for joy and fun and that is definitely worth our best effort.

Money Stuff

Money. We like it. We keep it in a jar on top of the fridge. We'd like to put more money in that jar.

But more importantly, money can be conceptualized as *energy*. Energy allows us to do other things we want to do. Energy is something we can share with other people. Money isn't a means in and of itself. Teaching our kids about money is teaching them how to use their energy in the world.

Start talking with them about how our society operates. You know, capitalism. And how the way it works in this country (along with other systemic social structures) has contributed to inequality. Help them learn responsible buying practices and teach them to do what good they can within the framework of capitalism. Take them to local farmer's and artist's markets. Shop local and small when you can, show them how to barter and share. Model ways that we can all use our creativity to make, DIY, upcycle, and program the things we need.

Growing up, Bonnie's dad *always* used to harp on the idea that "money doesn't grow on trees." He had a few sayings like that, but that one was really in frequent rotation. Little kids flat-out do not understand money. And it's hard to talk to them about it because they don't understand language like "payroll," or "budget," or "saving for a rainy day." Their frontal lobes don't understand planning ahead, and they like instant gratification. Hence the parent-tested favorite line about money trees. You, the grown-up with a budget, need concrete ways to talk to kids about this. Bonnie gives her daughter specific days when she can get something new. So if they need to run into the drugstore for a couple of things, Bonnie can say, "We are running in here for toothpaste and cat litter. There will be toys here, but today is not a buying day for toys. The next day I would consider shopping for toys is Saturday, which is three days from today." That really helps cut down the "But I really need this random princess car that lights up!" tantrums, saves money, and keeps that stupid random princess car out of Bonnie's living room floor, only to be stepped on later. As her daughter got older, the family implemented a system of doing a few things around the house in exchange for an allowance. Now when she wants something at the drugstore, Bonnie can ask her, "Do you have your money with you?" and her daughter can make the decision for herself if it's a day for buying light-up princess cars.

Studies show that kids pick up a lot of subconscious ideas about money, what it means, and what its importance is in our lives. They internalize the anger and shame that often accompany money management, and parents don't even realize those are the vibes they are passing around. So a proactive discussion about money and money management can head off those shame feels and increase your kid's overall earning/sharing/investing potential later.

Talking about money may lead to talking about career and life plans. What's your kid interested in doing? Will they need a degree or certification? How will the cost of that factor into their overall earning plans? Are they interested in something they can jump right into, or maybe get an apprenticeship and then get going? Not all of our kids will go to college, and there's tons of cool jobs that don't require it, so why take on the cost of a degree they won't use? If money is energy, talk about ways we can invest that energy in ourselves to make the life we want, college track or not.

Capitalism and Class

Because Bonnie has a lifelong love of politics, she often watched presidential debates as a kid. She can remember lots of references to "strong middle class" and the dreaded "Wall Street versus Main street" phrase that old-dude politicians love to employ during debates and speeches. Those phrases continue to exist in our language because class in America is a key part of life. The American dream is predicated on the idea that anyone can succeed; pull up on those bootstraps and make your millions!

The mythology of the American Dream exists in tandem with the fact that for generations, policy decisions have been made with the purpose of steeping particular communities in poverty and violence. For generations, the legacy of white supremacy and classism has been a key factor in policy and government decisions that have material effects on peoples' lives. The zip code a person is born into is a huge determinant of their access to quality health care, education, transportation, and jobs. Success in the U.S. is not just a matter of how hard a person works; it's a summation of generations of decisions that have brought us to this economic structure.

What has class meant in your own life? Bonnie grew up with parents who worked hard, and she had the ability to do most things she wanted, but her family didn't really take vacations or drive new cars. She had friends who did those things and more, and friends who did way less, and can remember noticing the difference in experiences around her but not really understanding what it meant. Ideas about wealth inequality and the 99% didn't factor into her consciousness until much later in life, but those experiences were real even without the vocabulary to discuss it.

Your kids will also notice those different experiences. How do you want to talk to them about class in America? How do you want to teach them to navigate these differences with kindness and without making a big deal of it? It's important to be honest with kids that this is a real and emotional experience for their friends. They may have a friend group of people with mixed realities; one friend might be able to afford the nicest prom dress or the expensive concert ticket while another friend is working a job to help pay the rent. Maybe your kid is the one who can afford the nicest prom dress; how will you teach them to be thoughtful about that privilege? How about if your kid is the one working to help support the family? How can they share that with pride while being honest about the stressfulness that can accompany a tight budget?

Make sure your kid has a wide range of ideas about how to spend time that include low-cost or free activities that everyone can attend and enjoy. Teach them to be inclusive and thoughtful about access to spending money and to do so in a welcoming way, like "Hey, my mom always buys lots of extra snacks in the summer. Want to come chill at my place and then we can head to the skate park?"

The reality of the U.S. economic system is that the majority of us are much closer to being homeless than to becoming millionaires. The system is designed to thrive when lots of people are just barely getting by. The COVID-19 pandemic exposed this reality in very clear ways, and has also shown how politicians think about support programs in the best of times. In Texas, accessing support like unemployment benefits, food stamps, childcare assistance, or rental relief is complicated as fuck. During the pandemic, some of those barriers came down, but the state was waiting with baited breath to be able to make it difficult again. Do you know how to access such programs where you live? Do you think it's important for your kids to know how to access those programs?

Bonnie has been involved for many years with a nonprofit that serves as a shelter and rapid housing program for LGBTQ youth, so conversations about economics and homelessness have been ongoing in her home. If the family has extra cash, it goes to that organization. If they have a chance to attend events or volunteer, they do. Because of this, her daughter has had lots of conversations about the lives of people who are homeless; she has some idea of how easy it can be to get to that place and conversely, how difficult it can be to get started from that place. Events give the family a chance to interact with the young people in the program and admire their ability to have perfectly winged eyeliner. Her daughter knows that the organization is working hard to empower and support those youth, and the family supports that mission. She knows her family isn't a savior to the youth or the organization because there's a community of love and support around the organization. It's a group effort she's proud to be a part of.

Environmental Stuff

There are a lot of topics that fall into a conversation about the environment and these will vary in relevance depending on your location and situation. The health of the planet is a feminist issue for many reasons; equity, sustainability, access to food and natural resources, viewing life holistically, and planning for a vibrant future for our kids and their kids after them. What are the ways your feminist family engages in conservation efforts? How do you view your role in planning for a healthier planet? What collective actions can you engage in (e.g., boycotts, purposeful purchasing, phone banking or letter writing, supporting specific legislation efforts, etc.)?

Food is a moral choice in some ways

Choosing a specific diet for your family, or your child choosing it for themselves, which is based on ideas about climate, vegetarian/veganism, and/or ethical farmworker treatment can be very personal. For many of us, in these ways, food is a moral choice and can be a lesson for our children in economic activism.

You may already have made decisions about certain foods for ethical reasons (like not eating meat raised in CAFOs). Teaching our children conscious consumerism is important. In this country, we vote with our dollars. And this is an entirely different thing than developing dieting disorders because a fashion magazine implied we should.

It's also important to understand that they may not follow this value system when they are outside of the home. And that's okay. If anything, it will reinforce the standard you are setting. Faith doesn't keep junk in the home. Both her kids learned early on that when they ate junk elsewhere they felt pretty crappy after. Both her kids are as lactose intolerant as she is, so their home was dairy free. Faith's son noticed that his acne would get bad if he had nachos at a restaurant. They started self-moderating in other spaces and were mindful that if they were going to eat something not great for them it was a special treat and they were okay with the possible not-feeling-great-after consequences. It worked far better than a moral absolutism that just made those items even more tempting, yanno?

Building a focus on sustainability

As you're focusing more intently on your family's sustainability plan and minimizing your effects on the planet and climate change, it's important to choose strategies that actually work for you and your family. Taking public transportation is great, if you live in a city where it works well and is safe. Start by looking at the available resources in your community. Do you have access to good public transportation? Does your city help you recycle, compost, or otherwise manage household waste in sustainable ways? Are there good thrift stores or buy-nothing groups in your area so you can lower your family's purchasing of new clothes or other items? How about local organizations that can use your kids' clothes and shoes, leftover art supplies, or books as your family outgrows them? Capitalism thrives on consumerism; to create a sustainably-focused family is to lower your role in capitalism overall and to have less of an impact on the health of the planet.

Now, we recognize that the small actions your family might make toward sustainability are not enough to offset the blatant disregard of big corporations for planet-saving practices. But, feminism thrives on collective action and building communities that are thoughtful and purposeful; your plan to lower your family's impact on the earth is an important part of that tradition.

Physical Ability and Accessibility

Here's a thing we can maybe all agree on: we all have a body. And those bodies are diverse and wonderful and strong in many different ways. Kids naturally notice diversity and are generally curious. That leads them to ask questions when they see people using wheelchairs or people who are accompanied by service animals. As parents, we want to encourage their curiosity about all the ways bodies can work or move, but we feel uncomfortable in the moment when our kid is maybe pointing or asking loud questions in a grocery store. However, to ignore diversity of physical abilities is to ignore the people living in diverse bodies, and we don't want that. So, start early in talking to your kids about people with differing physical abilities and non-visible differences that may be physical or neurological. Provide them with books, toys, movies and other media that is inclusive of people who think or move in different or assisted ways. Help kids (and other adults) to reframe our ideas of accessibility; a wheelchair, for example, is not a restriction. It's a tool that's available to help people move and live. Societal limits on accessibility are where we can focus our activism and support of people who use wheelchairs. Creating an inclusive society means we make space in our own lives for diversity.

In recent years, parents got really good at asking each other about food allergies. We all became very mindful that a few parents have kids who have serious reactions to peanuts and we started asking about food allergies when we planned birthday parties or neighborhood gatherings. Then we started just saying it when we invited people like "Come over for Aiden's seventh birthday party! We will have nut-free snacks and drinks. See you soon!" And then that started to translate to adult companions also; asking a friend to dinner started to sound like "Hey, wanna hang out and eat some food? What do you feel like, or do you have anything you're not eating right now?"

We can normalize this type of planning around physical limits too and make it totally normal and inclusive. "Come over to the park for Aiden's seventh birthday party! We will have nut-free snacks and drinks. And the park has wheelchair ramps and bathrooms with diaper changing stations. Let me know if there are other things y'all need. See you soon!"

If you're able-bodied, do your research about what's available in your community or where you can add your voice to advocacy work. If you're able-bodied and raising a kid who is disabled and you want society to do right by them, finding local advocacy resources will help you not have to have that fight alone. If you're living with your own disability, those things don't disappear when you live in parentland . . . having your own friends who joyfully make inclusive space is vital.

It's also important to create space for people with invisible disabilities too. People with autism, sensory processing disorders, or other types of neurodiversities may need different levels of accessibility as well. The important thing is to be mindful of physical diversity and neurodiversity in the world and to make space everywhere you can. This willingness can also be included in Aiden's seventh birthday party invite. Something like "This will likely be a typical seven-year-old loud and chaotic event so please don't hesitate to reach out if we need to be aware of what your kiddo may need to attend without being overwhelmed."

Faith's kids both had friends (sometimes very dear friends) with mobility issues, neurodiversity diagnoses, etc. We've always figured out accommodations that worked, and it was never a huge deal (e.g., when she was driving one of her son's best buds, he would switch to his foldable wheelchair that we could fit in her car). Faith has had mobility issues most of her life, and while she hasn't had to use crutches or the like in some time (*knocks wood*) she notices accessibility everywhere she goes. And if you haven't needed to, you may not. And it may feel overwhelming to think "This too?" but like a peanut allergy, it becomes another thing we learn to pay attention to. And it makes us more inclusive people *and* is good for our neuroplasticity.

If you're gearing up to be the person in your friend group (or your kid's friend group) that advocates for inclusivity and accessibility, be ready for it to maybe get complicated. That's part of the fun, honestly, like a logic puzzle. How will you handle it when one kid has severe animal dander allergies and another needs to bring their service dog to the BBQ? What about the kid who's a loud talker getting paired with someone with a sound-sensitivity? Here's a chance to use your thoughtfulness and creativity; the limitations of a plan or a space are just a problem to be solved. Ask what people need to be comfy, and start brainstorming from there. San Antonio has an amusement park that's been specifically designed to be accessible to all people; it's a cool place to visit and see some of the ways accessibility issues can be addressed to make a space fun for everyone. Bonnie and Faith can't wait to hear about your beautiful and flexible plans for Aiden's next birthday party.

Mental Health

General discussions of mental health are large and all-encompassing. For little kids, focus conversation on managing big moods, safe ways to deal with feelings, self-soothing, and processing verbally or physically when we need to. Older kids may need discussions about bullying, self-worth, asking for help from trusted people, or managing stress or perfectionism. Teens and youth might need support in processing their own mental health struggles, or supporting their friends, or dealing with the big emotions that come with life transitions. Many teens, if they are not themselves experiencing struggles with nonsuicidal self injury, depression, anxiety, or suicidal thoughts, have friends who are experiencing all of that and more. So your guidance here might be for your own kiddo, and it might also be for supporting your kiddo while they support their friends. You'll have to know the difference between supportive listening and guidance versus when to intervene, to contact other parents, or implement other safety measures.

Time heals a lot of stuff

When Bonnie was a teenager, she remembers having a run-in of sorts with some other girls and feeling really worked up about it. Her dad told her "You've got to be like a duck and let that dirty water run right off your back." She doesn't remember the specifics of the interaction, because enough time has passed and all of that high school shit gets left behind, but she can remember that guidance and still leans on it in adulthood. The point is, we see our kids hurting in the moment, but we have the wisdom of years to know that all this stuff will pass. We can acknowledge the hurts and injustices without stoking the flames of long-term resentment.

Faith's mom used to say, "They can fuck you over, but only you can fuck you up." (Faith realizes these stories make her mom sound like a crazy, chain-smoking, whiskey-slamming telephone operator as played by Bette Midler. Faith's mom would have you know she never smoked.)

In the moment, when our kids' feelings are hurt or they are upset about a bad grade, we can help them differentiate if their response means that something legit went down that needs to be addressed or if they are just butthurt on general principle, which is an important skill. They can take a step back, take a deep breath, and create the space they need to think about what has happened. Sometimes something hurtful needs to be addressed in the moment or soon after; other times it might be better to say "fuck this noise" and move on.

Often, the passage of time itself makes hard things easier to bear. Grief over a death or loss, sadness over a miscommunication or lost friendship, anger over a bad grade or harsh feedback from a coach . . . the impact of these lessens with time and support. Other hurtful scenarios call for forgiveness. Forgiveness does not mean allowing continued horrible behavior. It means letting shit go so you can move on. It's like the old trope, "Holding on to anger is like holding on to hot coals and expecting the other person to get burned."

There is far more power in just being done than in continuing to spend so much time and energy on being angry.

Never use physical violence in anger

We all have the right to live free from physical violence. Physical prowess should be used, as a last resort if at all, for protection of others, not intimidation of them. We have to talk to kids about how it's not okay to hurt people just to hurt them, or to use our physical power in anger against another human.

We know this can be complicated for kids, because frankly, physical violence can be common among our younger humans. They are fueled by their amygdalas, which can encourage retaliation when we are enraged. But we have to coach them in the difference between beating the shit out of each other for sport or middle school hierarchy, versus standing up for themselves in dangerous situations. Mary Karr, Texas shero, writes about how her dad talked to her about protecting herself from the bigger kids by biting them ("Lay the ivory to 'em, Pokey!"). But kids need to know that it's better to use our words, and to use our physical power as a last resort.

And when it comes to dating or intimate partners, no level of physical violence is okay. Our kids need to know that type of behavior is a deal breaker in a relationship and their physical abilities are not to be used against anyone they are dating, and no one should be using violence against them either.

How to fight a shark (or rather, what to be afraid of and why)

Bonnie's husband suggested this one, stating that he never learned how to fight a shark therefore never wants to go to the beach. Faith and Bonnie found this a funny comment, but it got us to thinking about the things we teach our kids about being safe in the world and the far more important things we leave out.

We grew up in the era of "stranger danger" . . . but no one told us that the people who might hurt us the most are those closest to us. Imagine if those of us who are now adults had been encouraged to speak out if we had ever been uncomfortable with or harmed by other family members, neighbors, pastors, teachers, etc.? We keep warning our kids about sharks, but not about the possible pedophiles in our families. While sharks do swim in the deep waters, jellyfish will come right up on the shore and are much harder to spot. Talk to your kids about the real dangers that can exist close to home and help them build their defenses. Which doesn't mean that sharks shouldn't be feared, but they may not be the most likely worry.

Building Your Community

Part of the joy of engaging in feminist or progressive work is that it's often a group project. When we focus on building a more equal and accessible world, it helps to be involved with groups of other activists, your friends, your neighbors, and other people who share your appreciation for progress. Planning our Feminist Agenda means having conversations about our goals and passions, our interests and beliefs. It's easier to be passionate when you feel like you belong to something and have common ideals. And it also helps to have collections of community members together so those conversations can happen. Showing our kids the importance of community, of finding people you click with and feel motivated by, means we also have to build a sense of community. We are all in it together so let's work together to build our humanity team.

How do you want to build your community? Do you have ways of gathering friends, neighbors, or other interested people together? What does it take to make those types of things happen and how can you involve your kids?

The importance of knowing your neighbors

We are becoming more and more isolated in our own communities. No one says you have to go to every neighborhood picnic (though Faith's neighbor grills a mean hot dog), but sometimes our safety and wellbeing comes from a community network.

Bonnie and her family live in a neighborhood that was built in the 1960s. Many of their neighbors are original owners of those homes and they are the sweetest little elderly ladies in the world. Nosy as hell, but with the best intentions. They watch the house during the day while we work, they bring over little snacks, and tell us stories about the old days in the neighborhood. We met these ladies by walking around to the houses around us and introducing ourselves when we moved in. We exchanged phone numbers and then they started bringing the snacks.

One afternoon, one of the ladies fell in her backyard. Her friend whom she talked to on the phone every night couldn't find her, so she came over to Bonnie's house for help. Bonnie's husband went searching and found the neighbor in the backyard, where she had lain for hours. In that situation, it was actual life and death that we knew each other.

Teach your kids that neighbors don't have to be our best buddies, but we do owe it to each other to keep an eye out for one another. Talk with kids about making polite small talk with neighbors, checking in occasionally, and celebrating holidays with little thank-you cards. You can start by baking some cookies together, then bringing them over and introducing both of you "Kidperson and I were on a baking spree. We thought it would be a good time to come over and say hi since we could share the love. Hi! I'm Faith and this is my Kidperson!"

Meet your neighbors. Take good care of them. Let them take good care of you. Make the world safer and friendlier right outside your door.

How to host a party and make people feel comfortable

Okay, so you're ready to start your feminist book club and the first meeting is coming up. You're putting yourself out there as a community-builder and welcomer of progressive peoples. What an honor, bringing new people together for an exchange of ideas and lots of cheese consumption. You look around and it seems like people are clicking! Conversations are happening! Phone numbers are being exchanged! Cheese is being consumed! Hooray! But wait; here comes your kid like, "Why all these people got their shoes on?! We don't wear shoes on the carpet!"

Now the vibe is awkward and you're going to have a lot of leftover cheese cubes.

We all have day-to-day rules to make our households function more easily, like taking off our shoes at the door to reduce dust (Is that just Bonnie that is a total freak about that? Faith says yes, but she has a Roomba so she doesn't have to worry about the dust build-up as much), but those same rules can be really awkward for guests, and our kids need to know the difference.

So, before the next time you manage to get your shit together to host a lovely New Year's Eve party, or clothing swap, or 'packing backpacks for refugees' gathering, discuss the ways you bend or alter your normal house rules to help guests feel welcome. Explaining "Our friends are showing up and we will let them keep their shoes on; it's more comfortable for everyone" will hopefully help you avoid the earlier scene.

When everyone feels welcome and comfy, the connections can be made and the new ideas can flow.

Manners for visiting other people's homes

At the same time, we need to talk to our kids about the manners they need for visiting other people's homes. This is an important lesson in following social cues, asking for guidance, and being a courteous and thoughtful person. We may not always agree with or follow other people's standards, but on their turf we can respect anything that isn't harmful. And learning the customs and traditions of others is a really beautiful way to help broaden our children's understanding of the world and how other people think and interact.

Prepare them ahead of time for what it may be like. Teach them etiquette shorthand—use a hell of a lot of silverware at a formal dinner even if you are a plastic spork crowd. Start with the utensil that's furthest out from the plate and work your way in. Encourage them to watch what others are doing and self-correct. Coach them to look for visual cues (like a stack of shoes next to each door or a set of coasters on the table) or to ask politely for guidance, "Is it okay to keep my shoes on in here?" or "Do y'all have any coasters? This table is gorgeous and I don't want to mess it up."

There are boundaries between what feels uncomfortable and what is unsafe. Taking off your shoes might feel awkward but is probably okay. Taking off other clothing is not okay. For kids anyway. At whatever types of parties you adults go to it's totally fine.

When Differences Matter and When They Don't

Diversity is beautiful and happy; the differences that exist between us as far as faith, appearance, or social class shouldn't be a barrier to forming new relationships.

However, differences can matter if they relate to safety. We do a disservice to our children when we insist, for example, on being colorblind in a world that isn't. And they need to be prepared to navigate those situations.

Faith's son has a very dear friend who happens to be quadriplegic and has other medical issues, including a seizure disorder. Her son would want to plan outings for them to do movies, dinner, video games, etc. And that's awesome. But Faith would have to remind him and help him plan around his friend's needs . . . making sure they were moving around places he could maneuver his chair, staying out of the sun, and discussing with his friend how to navigate barriers should they come up. (They've been friends for so long, Faith's son will simply pick him up and carry him if he needs to get somewhere that isn't accessible by chair, but not everyone will be down for that.) Does being a quadriplegic matter in terms of him being a good friend? Not a bit. Does it matter when they are hanging out and want to make sure everyone is able to have a good time? Absolutely.

We want our kids to have diverse friends and be accepting of many worldviews. And we can curate that by offering them diverse toys, books, and media to broaden their worldview. There are tons of great books out there about diverse families and relationships. There are books about boys who like sparkly skirts and women who have persisted through sexism. There are movies, TV shows, and songs made for kids which introduce diversity. As Sally Ride once said "You can't be what you can't see," so seek out diversity for your kids so they value different worldviews and can imagine themselves and their friends in all kinds of jobs and scenarios.

And even though they will choose their own crowd as they age away from us, we can still reiterate certain core values. Our hope is that everyone who hangs out with our kids needs to believe in the universal right to safety; they need to support the idea that everyone's life has value and is worth protecting. It may mean conversations or setting limits around the time they spend together.

For instance, Faith's oldest kiddo had a friend that was lovely to them (as well as to Faith), but had a tendency to say things that were . . . okay, straight-up racist af. Faith had a convo about it with her older kid, "I know friend-person is really lovely to you and always polite to me, but she also says things that don't align with my values and how I raised you. Something to think about in terms of your interactions with her. And I definitely don't feel comfortable with her being in my home, because that could end up with other people who have been invited into my home being uncomfortable because of her behavior." Read: I want my home to be a safer space for people and I'm not risking friend-person disrupting our peace.

Faith never did well with her parents insisting that any of her friends were shit, and didn't want to push that onto her kids. And Faith wanted her kiddo to make thoughtful decisions about relationships and boundaries in their own life. By demonstrating her values in action rather than insisting theirs be the same, it created a thoughtful space where Faith's kiddo didn't feel defensive of their relationships, but instead thought more deeply about them. Hopefully, anyway.

Practice of Cultural Traditions

This may be ethnic culture. Religious culture. Maybe it's just your family culture. But having tradition creates security and meaning in everyday life. Human beings are really wired for ceremony. If the tradition is Friday nights we go out for burritos, that's just as sacred as a First Communion ceremony.

Discuss these traditions in practice. Talk about the why. Talk about the history of the practice. Let them see that it isn't random, but is steeped in real tradition. When Faith's kids were younger, Burrito Friday was the one day where they were all home early enough to go out to dinner and no one had to get up early the next morning. It's also nice after a long week to not have to cook or clean up, and they are all burrito fans. But more than just getting a burrito with extra guac, she loved looking forward to time with her kids when she got to hear about their week and just hang out and chill without other shit going on.

Discussing and exploring cultural traditions in a wider sense is important to help kids have a broad understanding of the world and the ways we are interconnected. All people feel joy, and grief, and kinship. The ways we mark these experiences are beautiful and fascinating. How does your family welcome a baby? Is it different from the way your neighbors welcome a baby? What about grief and celebrations of life?

Sociologist Émile Durkheim wrote about this concept as "collective effervescence," humans coming together at a specific time and place to share thoughts and actions. Belonging to something beautiful and important and participating in cultural experiences is a wonderful part of being a human. What collective effervescence does your family celebrate?

Understanding Family Cultures and Differences

Not everyone your kid meets is going to have woke parents. Not everyone your kid meets will even have adequate parents. Part of building community is understanding everyone's at different levels, and we want to be as understanding as we can be about those differences. We want our kids to be kind, thoughtful, and nonjudgmental (when possible) in their interactions with other people's family members who don't show the same levels of wokeness. There is a delicate balance here between being kind while holding their authenticity around their own ideas and convictions.

Let them know that you'll support them if they choose to engage in tough conversations with other adults. Remind them to stick to the principles of keeping a level head and a curious approach to tough conversations. Teach them some gentle start-ups, like "I hear what you're saying, but that hasn't been my experience. Can you explain some more?" Teach them it's okay to walk away from conversations that feel unsafe, judgemental, or aggressively patronizing. When it comes to "controversial" ideas, progressives work to change people's hearts and minds one at a time. But that might mean uncomfortable and difficult conversations with adults who don't want their hearts changed. Eradicating racism, homophobia, misogyny, transphobia . . . these are worth the backbone it takes to have tough conversations. We owe it to our brave and passionate kids to cheer for the courage of their convictions, as well as their ability to know when to walk away from adults that can't hear it and can't keep them safe.

DEVELOPING SKILLS FOR GROWN-PERSON HUMANING (YOU KNOW, ADULTING)

The word adulting, like the word woke, has become overused to the point of irritation. And yet, the struggle to do these important grown-up-in-modern-society things continues to be a struggle for most people. Like, "How do I put air in my tires?" or "How do I make a doctor's appointment to talk about antidepressants when I don't know how to make a doctor's appointment even when I'm not depressed as fuck?" And on the macro level, how do we make the world safer, better, and kinder (and more woke) when we still can't figure out the public transportation app?

Teaching tasks like this to young activists means they can have more energy and brain power to devote to the bigger issues of the world. Even the wokest among us has to be able to stick to a budget at the grocery store.

Day-to-Day Life

A key piece of feminism as we understand it is the idea of equity. What can we do to lay a groundwork that's more equitable than what we may have experienced growing up? We think a simple place to start is to empower your kids to be able to manage their own day-to-day tasks. Even though this may seem pretty basic, it's powerful to teach self-reliance and efficacy. Managing your own laundry or understanding public transportation helps equalize; there's less of a privilege gap in knowledge of basic tasks, which in turn helps our kids avoid shame or embarrassment of not knowing the basics. Over time, these basics become routine, and there's peace in routine, but there's also space in routine. Once we have a solid routine, we have more headspace for the bigger issues and ideas rolling around in our heads and in society. Then, as our kids take this equity into their own relationships, they are more likely to have a healthy and functional division of household, emotional, and relational labor. The understanding of basic tasks sets our kids up for success and is part of a holistic view of people and life.

How to Write a Resume/Do a Job Interview

This is seriously an art. We can all make a basic resume by downloading templates from the internet; that's how Bonnie made her first resume (thanks Google, for knowing what neither peers nor parents did in that situation!). However, there's likely some people in your social circle who will help you make a good-looking resume that will stand out from the rest. Take time to find that person who's good at that design stuff, because a stand-apart resume can help your kid get a *better* first job, which means higher lifetime earning potential forever. And now that freakin' *every* job has an online application process, it matters even more. You can't walk into a grocery store dressed neatly, with good eye contact and a handshake, and walk out with a job. We have to represent on paper to even get a shot at representing in person.

To help your kid prep for a job interview, start by helping them pick the right clothes for the interview. Then brainstorm some questions they may be asked. Toss those out to your kid and let them fumble around with the answers until they settle on something that sounds okay for them. A few ideas to get you started:

- How did you hear about this job and what made you interested in it?

- What are your strongest qualities related to this job?

- Walk me through the steps of helping a customer at this job.

- If you could be an animal, what animal would you choose and why?

- You learn that a coworker is doing something that's against policy. What do you do?

Even little kids love talking about jobs and work. Bonnie's daughter loves to pretend with her play kitchen and cash register that she's running a grocery store/bakery hybrid (incidentally, the prices at her store are very steep; $950 for a muffin and some laundry detergent?!). While she plays, Bonnie will ask her some questions like "What's your favorite part of working at a grocery store? How did you make this delicious coffee? What makes you good at this job?" It builds kids' confidence to focus on their creativity and strengths, and that's what they need in a job interview down the line.

Proper Handshake and Eye Contact Guidelines

A good handshake is important everywhere, job interview or not, and is basically firm and not awkward. It's not a "how strong is your grip" competition nor a chance to do your best hand-puppet impersonation of a dead fish (which is the grossest thing ever, y'all). It's not a time to do a Will Smith/Fresh Prince impersonation either. Hand out, smile, direct eye contact, firm shake, let go. A good handshake can help in theory, avoid the clumsy "Is this gonna be a handshake or a hug?" thing because they are coming in strong with the solid handshake. (We aren't promising that the hug thing won't happen. People are cringey sometimes.) Take time to practice business/first impression handshakes by doing the extremes (hand crush vs. dead fish) and then finding something in the middle. Eye contact should be brief but not shifty; aim for maybe five to ten seconds of eye contact and then glance around. We want our kids to find that space between *who, me?* and *trying to stare into the other person's soul.* Add appropriate head nodding so you don't look like C-3PO and you're golden. This is practicable too; stare at your kid until it feels too weird for them. Then they know where C-3PO territory begins and ends!

However! Now we've all been living in a global pandemic where no one is shaking hands or hugging or anything else closer than six feet. The idea of having and/or needing a strong handshake might be really different in a couple of years. We might want to add some practice around phone or online interview skills as well as managing things like handshakes and eye contact. It's a lot to juggle, and may be more challenging for people in your family if you've got neurodivergent folks. These skills are teachable and practicable for people all along the neurodiversity spectrum. If your kid is neurodivergent, offer them the coaching you've used to help them navigate other social scenes; you know what works for your kiddo. And if you are a neurodivergent parent, you may decide you want some backup in this discussion. It's nice to have a range of experiences when teaching something like this that can seem overtly simple, but in practice, has many variables and nuances. If you don't live with neurodiversity in your home, it's still worth a discussion about how other people may be unsure of a social interaction like this and help kids brainstorm some ways to make this feel more natural for everyone. Bonnie reminds her daughter really often that people don't all process the same and sometimes facial expressions or other nonverbal cues land differently for people they are interacting with, so it's nice, particularly when meeting someone new, to verbalize what she's thinking and ask for consent with interactions. Something like "Wow, it's great to meet you! Would you like to shake hands?" is super simple and helpful. Bonnie has seen her use this type of interaction at places like playgrounds and museums; "Hi! I think it looks fun to climb up to the top of this, but we need to take our shoes off. Are you okay with doing that right now?" Which tracks, because most elementary school kids aren't necessarily shaking hands. But her daughter can take that style of comfy and inclusive intro into many experiences in her life.

Once our kids have managed to practice all this, we need to talk more generally about how handshake and eye contact norms vary vastly across cultures, communities, and countries. And part of building a more diverse world is learning about those norms and doing what we can to navigate those in ways that help others feel comfortable and accepted.

This is especially an important skill for kids who didn't grow up with these kinds of cultural norms. Faith's kids didn't. They grew up with an Indigenous value system. That you don't make eye contact with adults, because it's disrespectful. So handshake lessons were a really important thing, especially for her son. They made a game out of it, called (seriously!) Act Like a White Dude. He even practiced it with his therapist, a lovely older gentleman who had also lost his father as a teenager, and knew how navigating adolescence without that can be so difficult. Honestly, this was part of a bigger lesson about how to code-switch from expectations in one setting to expectations in another.

An entire book could be (and has been) written about code-switching. It's something that most of us do naturally (though it is clearly far more difficult for individuals on the autism spectrum and individuals who have a social communication disorder, among others). The idea is a simple one. We behave differently based on our surroundings (people, places, situations). This seems counterintuitive to the message of "Be who you are!" but we are *all* multifaceted people. No one is saying be inauthentic. Or a suck-up. Whether we like it or not, all situations have rules of engagement, both written and unwritten. Being able to move from situation to situation and navigate them effectively requires a read on what's going on and what is expected of you in the process. If you are teaching this skill, this may be a good time to tack on some life lessons of how this is an example of moving comfortably in society. And effective code-switching allows you to get your wants and needs met within those situations.

Write Thank-You Cards

A thank-you note feels so rare, almost old-fashioned, which is what makes it so lovely and unexpected. A note for a job interview (Faith once got a job she was wildly unqualified for because she wrote one), a kind gesture, or even just simple appreciation for another human; the world needs more kindness and gratitude. A client told Faith recently, "I didn't do *X*, *Y*, and *Z* in expectation of slavish gratitude. But when I get a recognition and a thank-you it makes all the difference in the world to me. I feel valued and appreciated."

A thank-you note can be for anything. One year during the winter holidays, Bonnie asked her then-toddler what she would like to say to her teacher on the holiday card. She had a very lengthy treatise that boiled down to, "Thank you for taking care of me and teaching me stuff and letting me bring Tigey to school with me," and it was quite adorable. Bonnie let her write the note in the card for herself and then Bonnie translated it for her. Her teacher cried when she read it. We don't have to teach our kids to be genuine in their thankfulness; we only need to give them opportunities to share that gratitude with others.

Thank you emails, phone calls, or text messages are all obviously appreciated as well. Maybe this feels so important to Faith and Bonnie because they live in the South and their grannies were serious about all things thank-you. But it's an art to be able to show real appreciation to others in the world, and it can serve our kids in the long run, too. It's simple and a win-win.

How to Use Public Transportation

The ability to use public transportation is another art and an incredibly important life skill for kids of all ages. Because the reality is, not everyone can afford a car, and unless you are lucky enough to live in a walkable or bikeable community, learning public transit will allow them the freedom to do the other things they need to. The use of affordable, safe, and efficient public transportation is a key part of the cities of the future, and is pretty damn useful today as it is.

We are lucky in San Antonio to have a pretty decent public transit system. Looking up the routes and planning your trip based on when you need to arrive somewhere or are done with the area you're in is pretty easy. So Faith taught her kids, by showing them how to navigate the bus website, and pointing out the smaller details like the digit sequence that is specific to each bus stop so they could make sure they were on the right side of the road, etc. She would also drive the route with them so they could see where they would get on, transfer, and get off.

Bonnie did not grow up in a city with public transit and has not often needed it as an adult. As a result, she routinely feels unsure of herself when she does need to use it. A few years ago, she traveled to a protest with a friend (thank goddess for that friend, for real) who was really good at navigating the public transport of the city they were in. Bonnie would have had to just ask strangers or make a guess about which train to take, which direction, and what time to get on. And then she probably would have missed the protest and been super fucking lost in a city she was unfamiliar with. She already has a questionable sense of direction, and if you add the pressure of being in an unknown situation, and the shame of feeling uncertain about something people seem to innately understand . . . she would have spent a whole bunch of money on ride-share services to stay off that Metro of Nightmares.

All kiddos are different, and all areas of your state or city have different levels of safety associated with public transportation, but Faith's kiddos were bus-trained by early adolescence. If you have a responsible older kid who will be in charge of public transport while bringing the younger kid, it's still a great idea that the younger kid has the same basic skill set so they feel more secure about the process.

A few months ago, Faith's niece insisted that she had no need to take the bus. Then Faith asked "And how many times have your friends texted to meet them at the mall and you said you couldn't because you had no way to get there?" Niece was all "Oh, snap, good point." Now she has a semester pass, and is all excited to use it to take the bus to the amusement park (where she has a season pass) and can hang out by the pool with her friends while her mom is at work.

Public transportation allows people the freedom for a social life, the ability to work, and the ability to learn how to manage another societal system which helps increase their competence in general. And it gets them to their protests on time.

Change a Tire

This is a skill that all of us who drive cars will need at some point. Even if they have roadside assistance, there are basic car maintenance skills that we should all know. Adding oil. Inflating the tires. *Changing a flat tire.* Things that aren't difficult to do, and save tons of money (and valuable time in important situations). Maybe the roads are epically bad in Texas, but we seem to drive over nails all the fucking time here. Faith has roadside assistance, but she and her husband were en route to a board interview the last time a tire blew. Changing it ourselves got us back on the road and to the interview in time, when waiting for roadside assistance would have taken a good hour.

The process of changing a tire is easy, but the tools can seem daunting if you're a first-timer. Show your kid how their vehicle owner's manual (or online video) has instructions for using the jack and loosening the lug nuts. Show them where the spare tire is located in the vehicle and how to release it from its holder. Let them practice in a safe and dry place so they get the process down when they aren't under the stress of being stranded on the side of the highway with a blowout.

And if we don't need it to change our own tire, we can help our fellow citizens who *do* need it. Bonnie does know how to change a tire, because her dad made her practice changing the tires on her 1967 VW Beetle before she could drive it anywhere. But one time she was pregnant and got a flat tire, and was going to change it when a guy on a bike stopped to help. When she thanked him, he said "Hey, sometimes you gotta do some shit from the heart." See, learning how to change a flat tire can actually make your kid a better community member!

How to Pack for a Trip

We all have stuff. And we like to take that stuff with us when we go places. We might need it! And we don't want to buy a new one out on the road! (Yes, we know it's unlikely anyone will need our charger for an iPhone 5. But *what if*? Huh???)

Whether our kids are heading for a weekend with their grandparents or off on their first college tour, they're gonna need luggage. And not just a suitcase full of gummy bears (though on second thought, does not sound like a bad idea at all). They need to know how to think about their trip and what they will need to navigate it successfully (so says Faith who has so many extraneous pairs of professional heels because she sucked at packing for all her business trips and always forgot to pack heels and then had to rush out and buy more but now packs *like a boss*). How to think about layering, how to plan outfits around a pair of shoes or two so you aren't going all Carrie Bradshaw. How to pack extra shirts because THOU SHALT SPILL. What to sleep in when not at home (hint, not raggedy shit, because what if the fire alarm goes off in your hotel and now you're outside a downtown Fort Worth Holiday Inn Express in some very unfortunate old boxers). How to pack mini-sizes of your go-to toiletries. Being able to travel competently will help them feel more empowered in navigating the world.

This applies to every day packing as well though. Bonnie's daughter carries a gigantic backpack to school every day and they had thoughtful discussions about what to include that was useful and necessary. Extra pencils? Check. Laptop charger? Check. Mittens even though it's 82 degrees outside? Nope.

She uses the same backpack to visit the zoo with her bestie. Then it needs water, sunscreen, her refillable popcorn bucket, and her wallet. She's still unlikely to need those mittens though (why is she so attached to these mittens?).

Take some time to help your kids figure out what they need to carry with them. What's useful and necessary? Are they carrying those things safely and efficiently? Where are they going and what will they need? How do you decide what to carry around every day and how do you modify that based on where you're going? Packing for the zoo would be very different from packing for a protest, a concert, or a sleepover birthday party.

How to Clean a Dwelling

The places we live get dirty because we live there. Humans have to learn the right ways to clean stuff so shit actually gets cleaned. Not just dirty shit swished or moved around, or hidden for mom to find later when it's *gross as fuck*. Ahem. Not that that's happened.

Kids need to chip in on housework. This can be tough for many reasons. One reason is that some kids are stubborn and don't want to help. Another issue could be your own issues about letting people help you; Bonnie is a bit of a control freak who likes things a certain way . . . so letting her kid help clean up is a practice in letting go of some expectations. Little kids can help with chores like picking up any toys they got out to play with, putting away their clean laundry, feeding pets, and setting the table. Letting them do these things helps them build confidence and pride. As they grow, give them more responsibilities around the house, like yard work, cleaning bathrooms, cooking and cleanup, and doing their own laundry. This comes with a conversation about how everyone in the home lives there and contributes in ways that serve the family unit, and we respect the time and effort of the others who live in our home with us.

These conversations need to include discussions about responsibility to others, as well as any rewards you may want to give kids for helping. Things like allowances or treats (or lack of) are personal decisions to make within your family, but lay it out clearly for your kid so they understand the system. Most data suggest that people like to feel helpful, and for some kids that's motivation enough, but for many others, a positive reward will add to those happy helpful feelings and get kids more motivated to help out. This is not about bribery; it's about choosing an appropriate reward for a job well done.

Another piece of these conversations is the specific processes you use in your home to clean things. Do you have a tried-and-true process for managing laundry in your home, or cleaning bathtubs? If so, take your kids through the process of how you like things to be done, or how you have determined works best for your home and life, and increase their chances of meeting your expectations. And . . . if they have suggestions for improvements or changes, entertain them, because maybe you don't know everything, you smug adult.

Everyone in the home needs to clean things. Everyone lives there, everyone is making messes, and everyone needs to clean. It's a way we show respect for each other and our shared spaces, but it's also important that relational labor like this is spread evenly. It can't be on one person in a home to keep everything nice for everyone else.

How to Cook Five Different, Inexpensive Meals from Scratch

Feeding oneself is a pretty basic human need. Feeding oneself on a budget, without fast food, is a real skill. It is also a great "win friends and influence people" skill. Almost as good as being able to tie a cherry stem in a knot with your tongue.

Honestly, a lot of these skills are about preparing for young adulthood poverty. Any of us who have lived on the two-for-a-dollar tacos at Jack in the Box and *ahem* borrowed a roll of toilet paper from work, remembers what it felt like to weep with joy over a real, hot meal. Pizza isn't cute day in and day out.

Faith's older kid was pretty determined to never learn to cook. Until they got tired of eating Subway (they worked there so it was free) and called, begging for details on putting together a pot of spaghetti.

Bonnie's daughter loves to help cook, and really loved it when she was in the three- and four-year-old range. She had a little stool that she dragged over to the kitchen counter and said "What's cookin'?" like a tiny sitcom husband. Now, she can do simple kitchen tasks like mixing veggies in olive oil or rolling up cookie dough balls. She can add ingredients together and loves to stir things cooking on the stove. Once she used a plastic knife to cut "asparakiss" for a dish they were making together. She feels confident in the kitchen because she's watched her parents work in there, and they told her "yes" when she asked if she could help. That "yes" can be hard, if you're a nervous parent (*Bonnie raises hand*), or if you're in a hurry or whatever. But it's worth it to give it a try.

A huge part of feeling confident in the kitchen is knowing kitchen safety. So if we're gonna let them hang out with us in the kitchen, they need lessons in food safety, knife handling safety, avoiding hot oil splatters, staying safe around the oven, putting out kitchen fires . . . you know, all that deadly shit that can happen in the kitchen.

We aren't ending this section with the five recipes everyone should know, because those five recipes may vary greatly from family to family. We do suggest thinking about your go-to healthy and comfortable meals. And basic cooking skills that make creating endless meals possible. Like cooking grains and legumes, making veggies taste amazing, how to work with meat and eggs if those are in your diet, etc. Once Faith's older kid realized how easy it was to hard-boil eggs, it was like the clouds had parted and the angels were singing. And for the record? Faith likes to mash her hard-boiled eggs with avocado instead of mayo. That's an official recipe, that right there.

How to Stock a Pantry with Staples and Grocery Shop like a Pro

So Bonnie admits that she is not fabulous at this. But this kinda goes along with cooking meals from scratch. So keep pasta, rice, sauces, and canned beans and shit. Or even foods for those days where you're feeling more, "Fuck this shit, I ain't cooking no matter how much you think it's a good idea." Keeping peanut butter and granola bars and crackers and shit can be a goddess-send on those days. Because sometimes you are eight cents short for the two-for-a-dollar tacos and that ain't no joke. And, let's be real, an apple and peanut butter is hella better for you than some tacos that haven't seen a price increase in over a decade and just *can't* be made with real meat.

Once a week, Bonnie's family sits down and plans the meals for the next seven days. The kid gets input on what she wants to eat and she can check the fridge to see if she needs more yogurt. They talk as a group about how the meals go together and ways they can reuse ingredients to maximize the budget and the efficiency. The kid loves to go to the grocery store because they have carts that look like race cars and she gets to hold all the coupons. When they get home from the store, she helps put the groceries away and usually only drops a couple of things. They do this for many reasons. First, they want her to be interested in food and cooking. Second, it's important to them that she knows that everyone chips in on planning, purchasing, and preparing meals. Third, she looks really cute driving her race car cart and waving coupons at people.

One area of the grocery store where young people need a lot of coaching is the produce section. The joy of biting into a juicy, ripe, summer-fattened peach is a beautiful thing to share with our children. Help them experience it every summer by teaching them how to pick ripe, organic produce and stay away from hard-as-rocks-sad-bad peaches.

It helps to have a handy list of the in-season fruit and veg for your region because they will taste better and be better in quality. There's also the "Dirty Dozen" list of the produce that requires the most pesticides to grow. And then you need all the tips and tricks for picking the best produce; are you a watermelon tapper or shaker? Whatever your methods, kids love to learn that stuff because it's sort of funny to lovingly caress the avocados to find the best ones.

Back in the '90s, they used to give farmer's market vouchers in the summers for WIC families. Faith was working with teen moms at the time and was surprised that 0 percent of them were using their vouchers. She started asking why. Turns out that the areas they lived in were not known for great grocery stores (go figure) and they had limited experience with really good produce. She arranged her visitation schedule around the farmer's market schedule and started bringing moms to the market and showing them how to figure out what was in peak season, what to buy, and how to use it. One mom called her after their trip to say, "Holy *shit*, I didn't know cantaloupe could taste this good! *This is so good!*" She got really interested in food, started searching out the best produce options she could find in her area, and started to really enjoy preparing meals for her family.

How to Use a Library

Free books! Smart, revolutionary librarians! Buildings of civility and democracy! Free access to information!

During the pandemic, libraries were closed to the public and suddenly the community could really understand all the ways libraries were helping people. Libraries offer free internet and wifi, computers, printers, as well as fun programming for people of all ages. They are a place to cool down or warm up when the weather is extreme. A polling place for voting day. A meeting space for community discussion or crochet classes. A safe place for people to spend time after school. A quiet place to think or read or listen to new music. Clean restrooms. Summer reading programs. Free art supplies. Toddler story time. There seems to be almost no limit to what libraries offer and no one will ask you for a dime while you're there (unless you've got late fees to pay).

As the pandemic ends and things open back up, take a chance to reconnect to your local library. Look online to see what the safety guidelines are and what programming might be happening. Take your kids of all ages and introduce them to the librarians so they know what librarians can offer, like reading suggestions or how to use the library search function. Maybe your kid can get their own library card!

Bonnie's kid got her own library card when she was a toddler, which was a proud day but also sort of bullshit because Bonnie specifically remembers having to wait until she turned eleven to get a library card. Bonnie grew up in libraries, both public and school, and still hangs out in them whenever she can. Libraries are wonderful community-focused spaces, welcoming and safe. And libraries have options now that didn't exist when we were kids. The one by Faith's house has movie nights and game nights (they own their own Wii so they have the kids up and bopping about doing Wii sports games). Besides the in-house story time, our local system lets you call in to hear stories and call in for homework help. They have a digital lending library and a music download subscription that allows you three songs a week to download. A library is one of the last places in our capitalist society where you can go and no one expects you to spend money. Can you tell we get all verklempt about our library?

Because libraries are places that are maybe a little more low-key on the adult oversight/intervention, it's a great place to let your kids wander the stacks and see what they might want to learn about on their own. Bonnie remembers being allowed to do just that as an adolescent and it was a chance for her to find information on topics she wanted to know about but didn't feel she could talk about with adults in her life. That also means your kid could be wandering the stacks and find some stuff that's not age-appropriate (for example, that summer Bonnie was twelve and read all of Stephen King's *It* in a cozy armchair by the window) or maybe things you really don't like or want them to read (hateful rhetoric or scary topics, maybe). That is definitely a risk, but the freedom to explore the library mostly outweighs that risk. Do your best to have a general idea of what your kids are looking for in the library, ask them questions about the books they choose or topics they research, and keep your communication open. They might find something abjectly awful, that's true. But they also might find a way to explore gender, or race, or dating and relationships in their own time and way.

Let's talk about libraries other than the municipal ones we all think of. Show your kids other library options. Like the little free libraries popping up in neighborhoods. Or the ones created by local organizations. One of the ones that Faith really loves in her area is the one run by the local worker's union (she donates her zines to them!). A lot of cool shit like this falls under the radar, so some web searches and asking other people in your area about what's available is a good start.

Managing Health

This section is about caring for the bodies that carry us through life. It's about being a whole-ass person instead of a half-ass person. It's about taking good care of yourself so you have energy to take on bigger issues and ideas. Burnout and stress are very real challenges in progressivism. It's stressful to navigate our patriarchal, white-supremicist society while also fighting against it with a view of a better way. It can feel tiring and hopeless—a hill too steep to climb. And all that stress affects your health in real and serious ways. Our brains and bodies are not very good at managing stress long-term; we are mainly made for quick fights or fast getaways. Long-term stress creates inflammation, and inflammation like that is linked to hundreds of ongoing disease processes. So, if you're gonna fight The Man, and you're gonna teach your kids to do that too, you've got to create a base level of taking good care of your physical, mental, and emotional health. Parenting and activism are verbs and the cause needs you in your best shape to sustain the long effort.

Connect with your own body and teach your kids to connect to theirs

What does it mean to connect with our bodies? That's a big question and a different process for all of us. But in general, it means being in tune enough with your physical and emotional feelings so that you can recognize what's happening and make decisions based on those cues. Are you hungry or thirsty? Are you achy and need a quick stretching session? Are you sleep deprived or otherwise fatigued? Do you need to pee? Do you need to hear the sound of a good friend's laughter?

Slow down, take a few deep breaths, and ask yourself what you feel and what you need. Our brains can get overwhelmed and overloaded, and then they overheat and crash like an old iPhone. The process of taking a few deep breaths can turn down the heat, so to speak, and remind you that you've got the power to turn down the fire alarms clanging in your head.

When we are stressed and activated, powerful chemicals are released into our brains and if we make decisions in that headspace, they are likely to involve a lot of dickitude. You know in *Frozen* when the trolls sing that song about being a fixer upper? There's a line that goes "People make bad choices when they're mad or scared or stressed! Throw a little love their way and you'll bring out their best!" Those damn trolls are really onto something.

We all need a go-to calm down approach. Deep breathing, stretching, time out in another room, a soft blanket or toy, a step outside, a quick blast of our favorite music, cuddle time with a pet . . . there are lots of safe options that can work. Try a bunch of things and see how you feel. Help your kids try a bunch of things and see how they feel. Connect with your own breath and love and don't jump into the fray when your brain is in redline panic mode.

If you need help identifying some coping skills that might work for you, we invite you to (maybe, possibly?) therapy. We know that sometimes people feel squeamish about therapy, or they don't know what to expect from it. We think of therapy as a place where you can learn tons of new, weird coping skills to help you connect with, and regulate your body and emotions. You can learn those skills without ever talking about anything too painful or scary. And if you learn something new and weird and you're into it, isn't that great? Faith and Bonnie are both therapists with therapists. Not everything is deep, right? Sometimes it's nice to have the perspective of someone not living in that situation at that moment who doesn't have a relationship with you in another facet of life. Seriously, Faith loves being able to say, "Is this as fucked up as I think it is?" and her therapist saying "Yes, totally," or "Nah, not really. Have you had anything to eat in the past couple of hours, Admiral Hangry?"

How to manage your health and be aware of your body

Teach your kid to make their own doctor's appointments. Because you won't always be around to do it for them. Because sometimes they need an appointment for something they aren't ready to talk to you about yet. Because our children need to own and be responsible for their health.

They also need to know what medications they take regularly and how to refill their prescriptions. If you're not around to fill it for them, what are they supposed to do? Send a trained carrier pigeon around the city searching for unguarded medications? Seems easier to teach them to use the CVS app.

They need to be able to communicate any allergies or adverse medical reactions. They need to know their blood type. They need to know as much as you can tell them about family medical history. Help them figure out when they feel sick and the specific things they can do to feel better. Once, Bonnie was babysitting a kid who was all "My tummy hurts. Can I have my tummy tea?" and the tummy tea was just chamomile, but it was his feel-better trick. Each of us has to know what helps our individual bodies, and it doesn't always have to be medication.

Most of all, talk with your kid about trusting how they feel physically. If they are sick, or have a headache, or just need more rest, this is all part of knowing our own health and being responsible for it. Questions like "How do you feel? Where does it hurt? Is your heart beating faster than normal?" can help even little kids understand that our physiology changes in ways we cannot see, but are important to feel.

Bonnie's lost count of how many times she has said to her daughter "I think you're doing a little pee dance. Maybe it's time to sit on the potty for a minute?" and heard "No, I do not need to sit on the potty and also you can't make me because I'm busy!" only to watch her rush to the potty two minutes later in a panic. From very early on, we feel like our physical needs get in the way of the fun stuff. Even as adults, we try to ignore the signals we get from our bodies because, hello, stop interrupting this sweet-ass Netflix binge, body! We have to teach our kids that meeting those physical needs and listening to our bodies is an important part of staying connected to and honoring our bodies and the ways they serve us.

How to brush your teeth properly and general hygiene

A body is a place where a lot of germy things happen, they stink if you don't clean them and cleaning them properly is a process.

Hygiene can be a battlefield because it's a place where the kid has all the control, and they fucking know it. And even if they know that it's a good idea to brush their teeth, they know that adults can't really force them to do it, and man, do they go on little power trips over that. For some kids, a reward chart can help decrease the bedtime war games. So like, a little sticker chart with all the things they need to do, and they get a prize when they get a weeks' worth of stars or whatever. This works for lots of kids, Bonnie's kid included. They have a very simple night routine: bath, brush teeth and hair, put on pajamas. If she does all those things with no bitching or begging, she earns a smiley face for her chart. Ten smileys means a trip to the treasure bag, so every night counts! That works in their house, but might not be a good fit for other families. So find the motivation that works in your home, and then you can stop yelling/begging/cajoling at bedtime.

Talking about hygiene can seem near impossible with older kids who already think you are stupid af and need to stay out of their lives. Faith's kids were both pretty reasonable about hygiene, but when issues became apparent (cuz no one's perfect), she tied in a reward system the same way Bonnie has for her kid. They wanted cute clothes? Those clothes had to be taken care of, which includes not stinking them the fuck up. Replace cute clothes with gray sweats for a week and hygiene improves pretty fucking fast, trust Faith. She also would have them be part of the hygiene product purchasing process, noticing they were far more likely to use stuff they picked out over the stuff that the Mommy Fairy just left in the bathroom. She also tried (and gets a gold star for this one) to praise good hygiene when it happened instead of bad hygiene when it didn't. And if bad hygiene needed addressing, it was done with humor and a presumption that it was unintentional. Like "Dude, you smell like ass banana, practice must have been rough today! I'll hold dinner so you can grab a quick shower before we eat!" Faith would also try to head off possible hygiene issues at the pass by planning ahead of time. Like "Dude, I know you are spending the long weekend playing video games with your cousins in the pit of despair known as your cousin's bedroom. I need to pick you up at 3:00 p.m. for family dinner, so make sure you give yourself time to scrub off the pizza sauce, hantavirus, and general stank, and put on clean clothes before I get there, cool?"

Navigate Diet Culture without Shame

Were you raised by a Boomer? Boomers as a generation have been exposed to more toxic messages about diet, food, and weight than any generation before or since. And if you were raised by a Boomer or had lots of contact with them, you've likely absorbed lots of that toxic sludge for yourself. Diet culture is capitalism at its ickiest. It thrives on the idea of some "ideal" or "default" body, and those of us who don't have one of those ideal bodies better (1) feel really shitty about not being ideal, (2) try to manipulate our bodies into being ideal, (3) spend lots of money, energy, and time on that manipulation, and (4) make sure other people feel as bad as we do if they don't meet the ideal.

Gross. That's definitely not the message we want our kids to get from us, simply because we haven't unpacked it for ourselves, nor from grandparents or other Boomer adults in their lives. Diet culture is a swampy place that breeds lots of disordered eating, shame, and depression. How are you going to make sure you're not dragging your kids into that swamp with you?

Start by noticing you're in the swamp. What messages are you getting every day about your body or other people's bodies? Are you following diet culture influencers on social media? Are you constantly talking about food or your body with other people? Who benefits from the ways you're talking about your body?

Then take that practice of noticing a little further. What do you hear other people saying about food or bodies? Keep unpacking and questioning the ways you have been indoctrinated to feel shame.

As you start to realize the ways diet culture affects you and your relationship with your body, we invite you to aim for a space of feeling neutral. Diet culture teaches us to hate our bodies, to feel shame or even disgust about them. Those are feelings that won't go quietly into the night, so try to be neutral about your body. It's maybe not realistic to love every inch of your body every day, but neutral is safe territory. From neutral, we can go to gratitude for the ways your body lets you interact with the world. We can be thankful for strong arms for hugging, or loud voices that can sing David Bowie karaoke in the car.

Make some rules for yourself and other adults for talking about bodies, food, and weight around your kids. Ideally, all the adults would be in neutral-to-grateful territory. They will avoid labeling foods "good" or "bad" and they will avoid those labels for themselves when they eat. ("I'll be good and eat the salad." "I feel so bad when I can't resist the bread basket!")

The diet and weight loss industry is a big moneymaker and a key part of the economy. The messages are strong, pervasive, and ubiquitous. The industry took a bit of a hit during the pandemic, so you best believe it will come back stronger and more aggressively than ever. Are you ready to resist it?

Bodies are not something to be fixed. They are something to be cared for thoughtfully, talked to nicely, and lived in fully.

Movement you love, not exercise for punishment

Many of us have a very complicated relationship with exercise, thanks to diet culture. We may have used it as punishment for eating something, a way to earn something we want to eat, as justification for any number of rewards in our lives, and many of us are having to detangle our own hang-ups about exercise as we try to teach kids the value of it.

We may have been shamed about our lack of athleticism. We may have been very athletic and we've let that part of our lives go as work and family demands on our time have increased. We may feel intimidated by gym culture. Those are all valid reasons we get away from healthy movement. But moving our bodies is an important part of overall health and wellness. It keeps us physically healthy, but can also decrease symptoms of anxiety, depression, insomnia, and distraction. But using exercise for punishment (like your middle school gym coach might have done) is counter to all of those benefits. We can exercise without being trapped on a treadmill for an hour, sweating and cursing the person who told us we needed more exercise; we can hike, bike, dance, walk while chatting, chase butterflies . . . any myriad of fun and fulfilling ways to move our bodies.

Kids are, in general, already good at that perpetual joyful motion stuff. Encourage them to keep that up. Playing at the park? Definitely movement. If we teach our kids to maintain their joy of being alive in their bodies, we can probably rediscover that for ourselves.

This might mean that you have to drive them to twelve soccer practices per week if that's how they love to move. This might mean that you take a nightly walk around your neighborhood at the end of the day to talk and connect. Bonnie and her daughter often do a bedtime yoga routine together to help wind down for bed. The important part is reiterating to your child that body movement is not punishment and it does not have to be intense to be beneficial. Talk about how we can find joy in moving our bodies in ways that do not bring us pain, that are appropriate for our abilities, and that we try to do each day.

Movement is a place where we can rise to new challenges (like rock climbing) or something we can practice and improve (like dance). But it's also available to us as simple pleasure. What types of movement bring you pleasure? What are your feelings about movement and exercise? What messages do you want your kids to get about movement?

Eating all foods in moderation

When Bonnie was raising a toddler she often joked about how eating with a toddler is sort of like eating with a snake—they want to eat one type of food, in huge amounts, on Tuesday, and then not really eat again until sometime next week. Threenagers, for real.

As our kids grow, leading them into moderation is key. Bodies need nourishing food all the time and there's many ways to get that food, whether your family is vegetarian or gluten-free or dealing with nut allergies. It's about balance and moderation with no shame or guilt.

Moderation means listening to your hunger signals and figuring out the difference between real hunger signals and emotional hunger signals. Giving your body time to send the "full" message to the brain before eating a second helping . . . and then deeply enjoying that second helping if you are truly not full.

Faith had the hardest time for years with grocery shopping. Whatever treats she would buy would be all devoured within two days of going to the store. Which left everyone five days of nothing but carrot sticks. She started talking about it in terms of math with her kids. For example, saying there were enough granola bars for them to have one each day when they came home from school. She wouldn't yell at them for having two, but there wouldn't be one available on day seven if they did so. This approach deflated the snack wars, and her kids moderated *themselves* way better because doing so was now their choice.

Further, our kids need to know that we are not good or bad people because of what we eat. Like, you're not superior because you skipped out on a brownie when someone else didn't. Being extremely restrictive with foods can breed an environment for bingeing. As long as everyone is eating nourishing food most of the time, indulging can happen free of guilt and it doesn't mean anyone is weak. Bonnie talks with a lot of clients who say things like "I feel like a bad person when I eat bad foods." No one's humanity or goodness is dependent on the ability to resist Girl Scout Cookies.

If you find yourself in patterns of eating that could be disordered or overly emotional, you're not alone in that at all. Because of diet culture, we've all been trained to be on one plan or another for most of our lives. Take some time to consider what you eat and why you eat it. Make notes about your emotional connections and relationships to food and eating. If it feels like too much to manage alone, reach out to a friend, therapist, or dietician for additional support. Most people know what it's like to have a complicated relationship with food. Keep a close eye on your kid's eating patterns too. Disordered eating can be easy to hide in teens and college students. Patterns like binging and purging, restriction, avoiding food all day so they can drink alcohol all night . . . these are all behaviors that can become lifelong habits that are then reinforced by our old enemy, diet culture. It's a terrible cycle and we deserve to be done with it.

How to drink and/or responsibly use substances

Because safety. Because social media. Because severe consequences. Because hangovers.

Bonnie and Faith live in Texas where it is legal for parents to let their kids drink, but be sure to check your local laws—you might be surprised! As Faith's kids have gotten older, they've been allowed a glass of wine at a family dinner or a hard cider at a family picnic. This has made alcohol something else that is out there and available and fine in moderation. Faith's son was invited to many twenty-one-and-over events before he was twenty-one because people knew he wouldn't drink without permission and wouldn't overdrink because, for him, it wasn't an exotic, naughty thing. If having beer isn't something that only happens on Forbidden Planet, then the temptation to have ten beers instead of one isn't as high.

Bonnie's kid obviously isn't allowed a glass of wine at dinner yet, but is already getting lessons in moderation and responsibility by watching her parents. Faith's father is a person in long-term recovery, so while he didn't drink, he made a point of discussing why he didn't drink and encouraged his kids to have a healthy relationship with alcohol (unless they found that they couldn't). He didn't want them to fear it because he is a recovering alcoholic. So if you have an alcohol-free house, you can still have the conversations, pointing out what you notice in other homes, in restaurants, on TV, etc.

The guidelines you want for your family around alcohol and substance use will be very personal and unique. As you're forming these guidelines, here's a few things to consider: your own relationship with substance use, the laws and consequences for substance use in your state, the risks and rewards as you see them, and general risk-reduction plans to make use as safe as possible.

Okay, what about drug use though? Deep breaths. Obviously the answer is a hard no, and it remains a hard no until they are at least 73 years old. Except it doesn't really end up working out that way, does it? And we have to have those conversations, too. What's out there, what's intriguing, what is dangerous, what consequences could occur, etc., etc. You can discuss recreational drug use without lecturing, right? Even if your hard limit is "just say no" you still don't want to shut your kids off or down, just as with drinking. Discuss why your answer is no, discuss ways to turn down drugs when someone offers them, always keep the door open for further conversations, *and* keep the door open in case something happens.

What if they decide to use anyway, and they end up high as fuck and stranded somewhere? If you've kept an open dialogue, hopefully they call you to come get them and they stay safe. Bonnie works with several families that have experienced that scenario; a few of them had a code word that signaled, "I need you to come get me right now and don't ask questions please."

There would be time to debrief the situation later, once everyone was safe and accounted for, but those kids knew that they could contact their parents and get the help they needed without a lot of drama. This way, no one feels they have to hide those decisions; there's room for mistakes and conversation. Faith's kids grew up with the rule that telling *always* gets you in less trouble than not telling. She would always eventually find out.

Okay, what if you use? And your kids know it. Take a deep breath and explain. Maybe you use edibles for sleep and they are legal when you do. Explain how and why you take them and that doing so is legal for you and not for them. Or if you are using something that isn't and they know? Then we get into the "How come you can and I can't?" Maybe it's the same edibles. Or you are microdosing to manage depression. Whatever. Explain that that's a choice you have made for your adult self with benefits that you have weighted against possible consequences. And explain that they can make those same choices when they are also adults, but that using now may actually end up having *more* consequences rather than fewer, and those consequences extend to the adults in their lives. That you could quite easily end up in the justice system because of their drug use, and they could end up in foster care because of it. It sucks, but it happens. At least in Texas. And it's okay to own, "I don't have a personal problem with you using X, Y, and Z, but the state does, which means my obligation to you is to say 'no.' When you're grown you can take all of our conversations about risks and benefits and make your own decisions. Right now, I'm the decider."

Take stock a few times a year of your own relationship to substance use. During the COVID-19 pandemic for example, there was a dramatic rise in alcohol consumption as we all looked for some way to manage our mounting pandemic anxieties. Most people will easily drop back down to pre-pandemic consumption, but some of us may have triggered relapses into more serious or heavy use. Be honest with yourself about what you're using and why so that your kids can see the whole process of responsible use.

Different approaches to self-care

Self-care is one of those therapy terms that's been co-opted by society and has at this point lost a little (a lot) of its real meaning. So . . . self-care isn't just pedicures and wine. Those things are great and can be part of our self-care plans, but that's not the end of it, right? Self-care means doing nice things for ourselves, soothing ourselves, creating safe spaces for our bodies and minds. It means taking care of the difficult tasks of managing budgets, getting life insurance, sticking to doctor's appointments. It means asking for the things and time we need to feel taken care of. What an important lesson for our children . . . that they are worth the time and effort of good care, all the time. Teach this by modeling caring for yourself. Ask for space when you need it, talk about the ways you take care of yourself and recharge, and be honest about the process. Reflect your child's feelings back to them. A toddler who is overtired and upset needs a reminder to take a chill pill; something like "When I feel tired and frustrated, I like to snuggle my blanket. Would you like your blanket?" For our kids to have a go-to soothing mechanism in a world that's tough is valuable indeed. For toddlers, this can be something like a timeout or a snuggle with a favorite stuffed animal. As kids grow, they can determine their own soothing mechanisms, like writing in a journal, doing an art project, going to the skate park, or solo time in their room. Self-care is a key way that activists and helpers avoid burnout, and as Audre Lorde told us, is an act of revolution.

A conversation Bonnie has with a lot of clients boils down to, essentially, "What do you like to do?" Americans are not terribly good at leisure. We are good at work. And many of us will work way too much, in our homes or in a workplace, because we feel a strong sense of identity in that sphere of our lives. Take some time to discover (or rediscover) who you are in your spare time. Do you have a hobby you enjoy? Are you taking the time you need for yourself to feel like a whole person, not just mom, dad, employee, business owner? What do you need to add to your life to make your self-care identity just as defined as your work identity?

Sex and Consent

A key focus of feminism for years has been making consent mainstream. Sexual violence, coercion, pressure, and fear have dominated sexual relationships for a long time, and feminists have worked hard to shift that narrative toward safety, consent, and pleasure for all people. These are ideas that can be challenging for us as adults, because we might have grown up with messaging or understanding of sex as something to fear. We've all had to do some level of deconstructing our undersanding of sex and the shame that can accompany it. Many of us are healing from sexual traumas; current estimates are that every year, there are over 400,000 Americans over the age of twelve who experience rape or sexual assault. Child sexual abuse statistics are also very frightening, with thousands of children under the age of eighteen experiencing abuse every year in the U.S. We may be scared for ourselves and scared for our children, but we can turn that fear into action and education.

Sex is a complicated topic and talking about it with young people can seem daunting. We hope to empower you to take a confident approach to these discussions by focusing on education, empowerment, safety, and consent. Everyone deserves a safe introduction to their sexual life, when they are ready for it, and that takes some groundwork on the part of parents so our kids have the tools that will help them achieve that goal.

When to start

Afraid your kids will have sex too soon if you talk to them about it? Take it from two sex therapists . . . the opposite will be true. For Faith's kids (Bonnie's isn't old enough), sex was just another part of being human. There was nothing naughty or taboo about it, so using it as a way of rebelling didn't happen. Both of her kids expressed comfort with setting their own boundaries because they felt those boundaries were supported.

Faith's son went to his first dance in sixth grade with his sweetie at the time, who was an eighth grader. She wanted to make out at the dance and he said "Okay, kissing. But no tongue kissing because I'm not old enough for that yet." He also made sure her best friend, who was dateless, got to hang out with them, and they pooled their money to make sure everyone got snacks at the dance. This wasn't stuff that was discussed before the dance, it was all a product of the standards set for respect and boundaries and care for others within his family. He totally got it and decided for himself no tongue kissing. And being inclusive. And cheerfully shared all the details. Things that made his momma so proud.

Be open to questions and be ready to answer them. Or find someone who can. Faith always offered her kids other adults to talk to if her kids were uncomfortable with talking to her about certain topics. Sometimes you need to check in with someone who has the same operating equipment, you know? Our general rule is if the answer to a question includes really needful information, it's simply answered. If it is kind of a silly question, Faith goes with "I'm happy to answer that question, but you can never unknow it." She and her son were just discussing his horror at finding out what bukkake and a dirty sanchez was. He is far more likely to say "Nah, I'm good. Nevermind," at this point.

Also? Keep age-appropriate materials out and available in that regard. Rather than foist those materials upon them as they get older (reading *Where Do Babies Come From?* out loud at bedtime works great with a toddler . . . reading *Not Your Mother's Meatloaf* out loud at bedtime isn't gonna work with a teen), just have them out and about in the main living areas.

Is it possible to overdo it? Sure. Respect your kids' boundaries the way you want them to respect other people's boundaries. If they say, "Dude. I got it," then totally let it go. There is an art to asking a teen about their dating life. Faith has found it works better in the car (teens hate parental eye contact!) and with a "So, talking to anyone new?" as an opener.

For smaller kids, it's both easier (no sex life yet) and harder (because you're setting the standard for the sex life stuff coming later). When Bonnie's kid was a toddler, these conversations mostly looked like naming body parts with correct names, talking about body safety and consent, and avoiding assumptions about future romance or life paths. Bonnie's daughter knows that a vulva is called a vulva and a vagina a vagina. She knows that people like her teachers might help her keep those areas clean, but that is the extent of what should be happening there. When she asks questions about marriage or relationships, Bonnie usually says, "Someday you might meet a person you'd like to marry. That could be fun!" As her daughter came into kinder and first grade, she suddenly got super interested in the idea of "boyfriends" and who is dating in her classes. Because she had a good base understanding of consent and the different ways relationships can form and look, she's able to have fun with these explorations instead of feeling confusion or even shame for being interested in relationships and crushes.

So let's talk about the sex stuff

Adding sex to a relationship brings on new opportunities and challenges. And talking about it with children-people can feel nauseating and terrifying. Bonnie used to work as a health educator on a teen pregnancy prevention project. That job involved talking with teens alllllllll day about safer sex, healthy relationships, good boundaries, and birth control options. That meant demonstrations about proper condom use, and one time Bonnie had to say the sentence, "Let's agree we aren't going to throw the condoms at each other!" because teenagers are ridiculous sometimes, and condoms are hilarious, but also, ew. At least blow up the condom like a balloon before throwing it at your friend; don't just slime each other with pre-lubed condoms!

One thing Bonnie was surprised by when she did that work was the disconnect between the teens and the adults in their lives. When adult-only classes were provided, parents confessed that they were confused about their own bodies, had no knowledge of birth control, or needed resources for their own unhealthy relationships. Those adults and parents wanted very much to help keep their kids safe in romantic/sexual relationships, but did not feel equipped to have the necessary conversations. When teens were asked about where they preferred to get information about sex and relationships, overwhelmingly they said they wanted to hear what their parents and parental figures thought about those topics. A lot of teen pregnancy prevention work is about equipping parents and reassuring them their teens want to hear from them. So, Bonnie and Faith are here to reassure you . . . your kids want to hear from you on this topic. They want your guidance and humor and knowledge (in age-appropriate ways, obviously). They want to know they can ask you questions and not be judged. They don't care if you don't have all the answers; they want an open door and a safe space.

Masturbation and body exploration boundaries

We sometimes forget that our silence on a subject can appear as disapproval. And the crap we heard from our families is easily passed down to our kids if we aren't super aware of those messages.

Faith and Bonnie have both worked with so many people over the years that grew up in loving supportive homes that still got many negative, shaming messages about masturbation.

Masturbation is very, *very* normal and the healthiest and safest way for all of us to explore our bodies and our sexuality. Children will start touching their genitalia as soon as they realize that it is something that exists for them to touch. We should remind them that this is something we do in private (in their bedrooms or in the bathroom) but that doing so is completely okay. Faith has even been known to encourage grumpy teenagers to take an "extra-long shower" to relax.

Masturbation is a good tool to manage sexual desire and navigate our own bodies. It helps us understand that desire waxes and wanes at different times. Nobody owes anyone sex—our sexual desires are our own and not the responsibility of others.

We recognize this is a complicated topic for parents to navigate. Most of us likely have a private but complex relationship with masturbation. But we encourage you to engage on this topic because for many kids, their experiences with masturbation will be their first experinces with sex at all. And if parents tread lightly, these experiences can be shame-free and pleasurable, which sets them up for a lifetime of shame-free pleasure.

You may want to start early with discussions about privacy. Something like "We all do things in the privacy of our rooms or bathrooms that other people don't need to be a part of. But even private things need to be safe, okay? So if you have questions or whatever, let me know!"

What are the messages you received about masturbation in your own life? What messages are you consciously or unconsciously sending to your kids about the subject? What messages do you want them to get from you about masturbation?

Navigating consent

If one more person tells Faith that active consent takes all the fun and mystery out of sexual relationships she may actually lose her shit in a very public way. Keep your eye out for news reports about some small, crazy bitch screaming from the roof of a very tall building, okay?

Active consent is sexy as hell when done right. And, shit . . . if some of the fun and mystery is taken out but that also means the rape is taken out, Faith and Bonnie are down for that exchange. Conversations about consent are a hallmark of thoughtful people; assessing comfort and interest levels are powerful skills that will be useful in many areas of life.

We can learn so much from the BDSM and polyamorous communities about navigating desire through conversations with partners and potential partners about what is on the table and what is decidedly not. And this may be why research shows that individuals who engage in BDSM are more emotionally healthy than their vanilla counterparts. This doesn't mean explaining to a three-year-old when spanking is fun versus not fun, but it's a great resource for those of us who are trying to teach consent and boundaries to our kids when we weren't taught these skills when we were kids ourselves.

Conversations about consent exist in all parts of our lives, not just in the sex parts. Younger kids can learn about consent by controlling who they hug and when. They may learn about consent when they try to pet the cat and Whiskers scratches the hell out of them. "Kitty doesn't consent to petting right now!" was a very common phrase in Bonnie's house when her daughter was a toddler. Living things have free will; respecting consent means we give freedom to exercise that free will.

Those messages are the same as they get older. Who do you hug, and when? What level of physical touch is comfortable in a given scenario? How do you know the other person is consenting at the same level? One nice thing about coming out of the COVID-19 pandemic is how people now ask "Are we hugging?" instead of just going in for the hug. Consent is asking and respecting the answer before any move is made.

Conversations about consent need to define terms like pressure or coercion. They need to include discussions about consenting while using substances, like, what level of drunk is still okay for active consent? Also about how people can consent at the beginning of an interaction and then change their mind at any point, so we ask for consent frequently throughout an encounter.

Consent means saying, simply "Is this okay with you?" and checking in continuously to make sure things remain okay. When you're talking about consent, discuss how silence doesn't equal being okay. We need to ask for active assent in some way, shape, or form (whether that means nodding or a "Fuck yes, don't stop!").

Flirting vs. harassment

Harassment and assault have gotten a lot of coverage over the past few years, starting with Tarana Burke's #MeToo activism in 2006. As the conversation around sexual- and gender-based violence spread across the internet, online activism and stellar reporting exposed the actions of some powerful people and we suddenly all knew what we had known all along: harassment and assault are obviously unacceptable, but they have been happening in the shadows (and with help from hush-money settlements) for decades in American workplaces. This has been a painful and necessary national conversation and hopefully a sea change moment; include your kids.

Help them understand that flirting requires consent. Flirting is a two-way conversation; it takes nuance and attention to detail. Harassment is overt and obnoxious. It's the difference between being tickled pleasantly with a feather and being whacked in the head with a textbook. Talk about intent versus impact and how what seems okay for them might be really uncomfortable for someone else. For example: "When you snuck up on me and licked my hand, you thought it was just a funny joke. Your intent was to be funny. But it felt really yucky for me; your impact wasn't funny. Instead it made me feel gross. Please don't do that again." Discuss how there are places where consent for flirting would be possible, like on a date but not in a workplace. Bonnie is married to a teacher, and he talks frequently about the flirting/

harassment he sees in high school hallways. There's such a thin line between welcome flirting and unwelcome harassment, and part of navigating that is helping our kids recognize the need to tread lightly.

What would you do if your kid was accused of harassment? How do you want to coach them to interact with others to show respect for boundaries? How will you handle it if your kid is the one claiming to be harassed? What conversations and support do you think kids need at different ages?

What's flirting for one person is harassment for another. What starts as flirting can morph into harassment. Our kids need help navigating this. Honestly, this conversation has to be ongoing and has a lot of room for thinking out loud and working through misunderstanding. A lot of grown-ass people have trouble with these concepts. Start by asking your kid what they see among their friends, in school hallways, or what they've experienced themselves, and go from there. Go gently and with an open mind.

Not getting roofied

Dr. Faith's son was probably fifteen when she and Mr. Dr. Faith took him to a local bar to hear a band they all liked. He ended up getting two great life lessons that night. One was on the danger of getting stupid drunk (he saw someone fall over into the street and nearly get himself hit by a car along with his friends who were trying to get him out of the street) and the other was on how not to get roofied.

After we ordered our drinks (Cokes), Faith showed him how to hold his glass with his hand over the top and told him that if he ever leaves it unattended, to consider it unsafe to drink and toss it. He thought it was a joke, but we discussed what roofies are, how they would impair his ability to consent to sexual activity, and that men can be victimized just as easily as women. He still holds his glass like that, though he rolls his eyes when he does so.

Generally, to avoid getting substances added to our drinks, teach your kids to keep their drink with them at all times. They'll want to cover the top of it, just like Faith's son. They should get their drink directly from a bartender or server. They can stick with friends and have a system for watching each other's drinks. There's even cups, straws, nail polish, and drink test strips that change color in the presence of a sedative. Maybe someday, we won't need all this bullshit just to go and have a safe drink with friends. But for now, we can teach our kids all the possible ways they can look out for themselves and their friends.

How to find the right birth control

Birth control is such a pain in the ass, especially if you are someone with a uterus and are sensitive to hormones. Anyone who has a penis and a latex sensitivity can struggle, too.

Talk about options, both long- and short-term. This conversation needs to start early (probably earlier than you think it should) because you want your kid to be covered for pregnancy prevention before they start having sex. The conversation about birth control will likely coincide with the onset of puberty, although they don't need to be actively on a birth control option at that time. Just plant the seed that, oh hey, you're really growing up, and pregnancy is a thing that can happen, and there are ways to prevent it! Open yourself up for the questions, help them meet with their pediatrician, and plan to give them solo time with the doc at that visit. Your doc might know, too, of some community programs or spaces where your child or teen can learn about and talk about birth control with a trained sexual health educator.

There are also great websites, written for and by young people where your kid can get medically accurate information about birth control options.

It may turn out that your kid never engages in the kind of sex where they have to worry about pregnancy prevention. But you might not know that as early as when you need to start the birth control conversations. Even if your kid does come out as lesbian or gay at an early age, conversations about birth control are still vital. Sexuality is fluid, and at thirteen, they may think they are only into dudes, but then at fifteen they meet a dreamy girl, realize they might be bi, and now birth control could become necessary—or they're still only into dudes but the love of their life is trans. And even if they live lives where birth control is never needed, at least they have a good understanding of the options and can help friends by sharing that knowledge. There's so many reasons to talk about birth control. So go talk about birth control! But go gently and with an open mind.

All the other safe sex and risk reduction stuff

A few years ago, Faith brought her older kid and bonus daughter to the gynecologist. They both were looking at birth control options, and Faith had discussions with both of them about the options and what protection each options gave (e.g., no babies, STI prevention). The GYN was so impressed she asked Faith to have the same conversation with her kids. She apparently hadn't done so, and loved hearing how Faith discussed these issues. Faith was really surprised and hadn't really thought about how difficult that conversation can be for parents . . . even if you are a vagina doctor.

Cue 2017. Bonnie and Faith (along with their friend Aaron who is an MD on a college campus and therefore has lots of experience with STIs) wrote a zine about this, the *STI FAQ*. It's become a zine that parents are buying for their kids because the information in it is really pragmatic information (in a manageable size). If these talks gross you out, or you don't know all the details, find a good resource. Whether it be our zine, a similar book or zine, a trusted friend or family member, or a good YouTube channel. Bring your kids to a treatment provider if you don't have the skill set to answer all their questions. Faith has done psychoeducation (therapist term for sharing useful information) with several teens and preteens in her practice at the request of their parents.

How do you plan to handle it if your kid does contract a sexually transmitted infection? What will be your process for getting them regular checkups and testing? What if they experience an unplanned pregnancy?

The answers to those questions might be complicated for about a bazillion reasons. First, depending on your state, there may be laws related to all this business. In Texas, the age of consent for sex is seventeen, but the age to consent to medical procedures is eighteen. Also in Texas are a bunch of draconian abortion laws, sex education laws, and access to sexual health care laws. So there is a possibility that you'll need to know what the laws are and what community organizations are available to help you navigate them. The National Network of Abortion Funds has good info about a lot of these topics.

Whatever path you'd like for your family to take through an unplanned pregnancy, you're gonna need support. Abortion, adoption, raising a baby . . . none of these are easy for young people and each option comes with complications. What organizations are near you that could be useful? And now that you know about them, how can you support their efforts? Even if your kid never needs those services, other kids are using them.

Try out a sexual partner before committing to them long-term

Did we just say encourage your kids to have lots of sex? Not necessarily.

When people are new to sexual relationships, there is a lot to navigate. The chemical interactions in your brain when you're in a new relationship are complicated as hell. Add cultural norms, pressures, wanting the fairy-tale ending, and also mashing body parts together . . . that's actually more than a lot to navigate. Before we commit to a partner in a long-term way, we need to test their ability to communicate about topics like sex and sexuality, consent, and ground-level agreements (what we like, what we don't like, what are our relationship dealbreakers, how do we define this relationship, and so on). Bonnie, for one, really bought into that teen rom-com idea that a first-time sexual experience equals being with one person forever. But the other person in this story was a total turd for many reasons, and instead of acknowledging the signs that they were incompatible, Bonnie forged ahead with that movie-riffic belief, resulting in less than ideal outcomes. We can encourage our older offspring to experiment and look for compatibility with another person without some romanticized lifelong commitment.

Individuals who have strong value systems in regard to sex before marriage can still experiment within their moral boundaries to make sure that this person is someone they feel that spark with, can communicate wants and desires with, and enjoy being with.

The Internet

Remember dial-up? Bonnie does! She can remember the first time she heard that modem sound and the little running AOL guy showed up on the screen. There is zero chance in hell that little fifth-grade Bonnie could have ever dreamed what the internet would do to our lives. It's dog-eat-dog out there!

Bonnie, for one, is thankful for the internet. How did she ever find an address without Google telling her where to find it? How did she live on once-weekly episodes of *America's Funniest Home Videos* before YouTube gave her a constant stream of Stupid Human Tricks and Bad Lip Reading videos? She can't even comprehend that hellscape.

The internet is a lot of things to a lot of people. And our kids are living on it. Bonnie had a client tell her about how one week, she spent twenty-two hours watching TikTok videos. That's like, a lot of TikTok. If the internet is going to be this integrated into our kids' lives, we've got to talk about it.

How to be safe online

Oh sweet Buddha. This is a book in and of itself. But we can't seem to reiterate this enough to parents. Start this conversation early and have it often; this is an ongoing dialogue as the internet changes and your child changes too. The "Internet Safety Talk" mirrors in many ways the "Safe Sex/Birds and Bees Talk," namely in that it never ends and requires an open-door policy on your part to help keep your kid safe as they navigate new relationships.

Many kids play on tablets and phones as early as toddlerhood. Make sure you have the parental safety controls set in ways that keep your little safe and on apps and websites designed for kids. Stay close by and watch what they interact with and make commentary. Even the online spaces designed to be safe for kids can have questionable content (particularly if the site is mostly user-created content, like video streaming sites). Also, many apps for kids have in-app purchasing available, and it's really easy for your toddler to rack up a sizable bill while they play on their virtual farm. All of y'all have heard one story or another about a kid spending thousands of dollars on Candy Crush or whatever. So, when your kid is little, be nearby and nosy.

As they grow, continue the conversations in age- and maturity-appropriate ways. Talk about the permanence of things on the internet that seem to be gone, how people on the internet will lie to trick them, and how sending or receiving nude photos can be a legally punishable offense. Talk about the stranger-danger aspect of the internet and how they can have a healthy skepticism for who people say they are online. Process what it means to participate in cyber-bullying and help them look out for friends who are in danger of being on either the giving or receiving end of online meanness. Make them roll their eyes with irritation over how much you talk about this. That means they are alive to roll their eyes, so we still win.

Keep an eye on the ways they interact with people they know as well. Provocative or mean-spirited messages can get out of hand quickly. Screen time can affect sleep patterns and ability to focus. Time away from their dinging notifications is important. Help your kids set reasonable limits for the ways they interact electronically and also reassess on a regular basis to make sure those limits are working as needed.

You have to be firm but nonjudgmental in conversations about life online. You need your kid to know that you're a safe person to come to, no matter the question they hold. Set reasonable expectations about what your kids are and are not allowed to watch online and explain that these boundaries are to keep them safe and to make it so they don't see things they aren't ready for and cannot unsee. Talk about the pros and cons of social media and how to evaluate what they are posting. Questions like "Would you want that post read back to you in a job interview or in front of your class full of friends?" can be helpful determinants about the appropriateness of posts. Did you know the Library of Congress, up until 2017, kept and catalogued every tweet since the inception of Twitter? Yeah, internet stuff doesn't go away.

Being safe online also means we manage our time there responsibly. What time limits do you feel your kids might need to manage their online time? Are you okay with more time online in one area (maybe chatting with friends or playing collaborative games) versus other areas (like mindless games, social media, or streaming sites)? How will you enforce or encourage responsible use? Are you yourself engaging in responsible use?

"I saw this thing online . . . "

How many conversations have you had with that line? "I saw this story online about how bats can really turn into vampires and the lamestream media is just covering it up because they work for the vampires. Can you believe that?"

No, Cindy, we can't believe that. Because it's clearly nonsense. But with other stories and topics, it can be harder to tell what's real and what's vampires. How will you guide your kids through the process of finding real information on the internet? What process do you use for yourself? How do you stay on top of the ways that propaganda and image manipulation show up in your digital life?

This is seriously getting pretty challenging. It used to be easier to tell what sites are a rando's blog versus a reliable news source. But more and more rando blogs are made to look like those legit sources and it's easy to fall into them as fact.

Online misinformation is incredibly powerful. It can reach large numbers of people, be passed around easily, and be made to look exactly as someone wants it to look. We've seen it come into play in elections, in stocks, in managing a pandemic; people will believe what they want to believe and if it looks real, it might as well be real. And as we all spend more and more of our time online, the power of this information grows because it's more likely to make its way to our screens.

Some general questions to help our kids start to navigate this might include "Who wrote this story? Who benefits from the information in it? Can I find similar information on different sites? What does the librarian think about this website?"

BECOMING A
WOKE PARENT

Real talk: parenting is more than just raising your kids right. It's about learning to be a better person yourself too. Here we discuss how to learn for yourself, how to be open and better at communication, and how to take good care of yourself. A kinder, more peaceful world begins with all of us being kinder and more peaceful with ourselves. This section is begging you to do some work on yourself with compassion and, hopefully, emerge feeling a bit more free from the societal messages you may have absorbed throughout life. You're not going to overcome a lifetime of conditioning quickly or easily, but you can go bravely and boldly into new spaces by asking new questions and bringing curiosity to your own experiences. Move gently into this new and vulnerable space.

Respect the Identities of Others

Humans are complicated and beautiful creatures. We all have unique experiences and viewpoints and we compile those into our personalities and into the ways we show those personalities to the world. Because we live in a culture that tends to give lip service to "diversity" but in reality, makes people feel shame for their differences, it can get confusing to navigate.

You'll want to create a space where people are valued and respected for who they are. We don't have to agree with all of their choices or opinions; but each one is a human soul (or full of human goo, whatever your understanding), and we owe each other the space to exercise our free will.

Our kids need to know that they are safe to be who they are. That means other people are safe to be themselves too. The identities of others are not up for debate, ridicule, or disdain. In fact, whenever possible, the identities of others should be proactively affirmed by use of appropriate language or actions. Using names, pronouns, and descriptors can feel complicated to do without sounding like you're putting lots of emphasis on how a person looks; but using those words is powerfully affirming to people when you do it right.

When everyone is free to be who they are, they also get to define themselves with pronouns and descriptors, and we have to teach our kids to respect the ways people identify. And we need to talk about the process of reclaiming words, who those words belong to, and how to navigate those conversations. In Bonnie's clinical practice, she works with patients who are exploring weight-loss surgery. If she sees five patients in one day, she will hear the word "fat" used in five different ways. Some people use it proudly or factually; others speak the word with shame. An adjective/identifier word like that is very personal and is colored by very personal experiences. We owe it to each other to listen, to understand pronouns and identifiers as what they are: personalized definitions of lived experiences. And we don't have to call each other out on using words that may seem pejorative at first.

Turn on your compassion and listen to the experiences of the people who are sharing their identities, and recognize when words are used with pride, or even defiance, versus when they are used in ways that feed self-hatred and doubts. A person might say "I identify as fat because that's a powerful word." Or they might say "I feel judgmental eyes on me all the time because I am fat and I hate it." Those are very different experiences, and may even come from the same person. It's not our job to define the experiences of others. Our job is to listen, to ask for clarification, and then honor the process another human has gone through to define themselves.

If you get it wrong, for example using incorrect pronouns, acknowledge it but don't make a big deal out of it. A simple "oh, I slipped there and used the wrong pronoun; I'll be more mindful" can go a long way. But if you slip and harp on it, the experience can get very awkward. It's likely the person you're talking to is ready to move on, and if you launch into "They/them is just really hard for me because it's a use of grammar that doesn't make sense in my head and wow I'm really trying but it's super hard for me!" not only have you brought more attention to the situation, you're being disrespectful. You're telling them that *they* are making life hard for *you*. When they're just existing in the world and want to be seen authentically. Worse, if you slip, apologize, and then keep slipping, the interaction will start to feel aggressive. We can show each other grace for a misstep; we cannot let those missteps become microaggressions that make people feel unsafe. Try to practice on your own, watch videos and read more about why it is important and valuable work. If you struggle with it, or find another friend who is struggling and practice together!

What descriptors do you use for your own identity? What about your family and friends? Do you feel a mutual respect for your identity and those around you? How can you be more affirming of others' identities?

How to Listen to Understand Instead of Respond

Take a moment and think about what it was like to have a conversation with your parents when you were younger. Whether the conversation was light or heavy in topic or tone, did you feel heard and welcomed? Were your opinions solicited? Were the emotional undertones seen and acknowledged?

Or did you grow up in a family where "Kids are seen and not heard," or "You don't know; you're just a kid" were the basic beliefs? Or maybe whatever point you made was rebutted swiftly and unceremoniously?

Were you allowed space to vent and think out loud, or were the adults in your life quick to try to rescue or problem solve?

We all model the communication we grew up with, to some extent. There are parts of that which work and parts that don't, but to be able to actually, truly listen to another person is powerful. For your kid to feel they are understood by you creates a strong attachment and safe space for all kinds of conversations, particularly the ones we are discussing in this book.

What parts of your childhood communication lessons do you want to carry on and what do you want to leave behind? What conversations can you remember where you felt valued and affirmed? What about shamed or misunderstood?

We don't get anywhere in any conversation if we are waiting for the chance to land a verbal TKO. This world needs more (attempts at) understanding and less talking like we are in an online comments section. Tough topics don't need a "devil's advocate" or other adversarial approaches like mockery or condescension. (Though a well-placed joke is a strong way to diffuse tension, jokes can also derail a conversation and be used as a way to avoid a topic altogether; use humor sparingly.)

Listening is an art, which requires empathy and creativity, both solid life skills for our little Padawans to learn. Truly listening to another person means you can identify (1) the content and words of what is being said, (2) some of the processing the person went through to choose the words they use, and (3) the emotional meaning behind what is being said.

There is a cheesy-but-reliable therapist trick for teaching empathic listening. When two people are in conversation, one person holds a physical object like a pillow or a TV remote or whatever is handy. The person holding the object gets to talk while the other listens. Then, the "listener" offers their understanding of what was said by the "speaker." When the speaker feels heard and understood, they can pass the object to the listener and the roles switch. If the "speaker" doesn't feel understood, they can continue holding the object and they can re-state their position or rephrase for better understanding. Then the "listener" can try again. This is not a time for the "listener" to offer rebuttals, explanations, or defenses; it's a time to listen for content and feelings.

Typically, it takes about three rounds to get to the guts of the conversation, which is where you find the feelings, implicit bias, and beliefs. It's really interesting to do this exercise with people in your life, and your kid will like it because they will have all of your attention.

For example:

Parent: It's time to put on your clothes for school!

Kid: I hate those clothes! I won't do it!

Parent: That's a strong feeling. Can you tell me more about that? What's going on?

Kid: Nothing, but I'm not putting on any clothes. I'm not going to school today.

Parent: Help me understand; you always love school. Are you maybe feeling a little nervous about your recital this afternoon?

Kid: Ugh, yes. And I am not ready to get dressed and go to school because then the recital will be there.

Really listening to another person gives us a chance to offer support and build deeper relationships and understandings with others. This also means we need to put aside our need to be right all the time, because, actually, no one likes a know-it-all. Which is bad for Bonnie and her kid because they think almost every situation needs a "Well, actually . . . " But actually, people don't want your advice (even people who are asking for it, which is confusing, we know, but whatever). People want to feel heard and supported, actually, and being able to be that person for someone is a valuable human experience.

Instead of "Well, actually . . . " try some phrases like "That's interesting" or "What makes you think this?" or "How can I support you?" or "Tell me more about that" and then actually listen when your kid answers.

Bullies Come In Many Forms

Most adults know what it's like to face a bully. That dickhead in traffic cutting you off and then yelling at you. The shitty boss who undermines and gaslights you. The online trolls who threaten to burn your house down because you shared a list of reasons Texas is the best state (it's not, we know it's not, don't doxx us, kthnx).

Imagine how much harder those types of interactions are for a kid; feeling small and even more helpless in the face of a ragey and mean person, who is probably not a stranger, but is in fact the person who sits behind them in math class. We have to coach our kids in the ways they can stand up to bullies, while keeping themselves as safe as possible, and while keeping their own moral compasses intact.

Start by coaching them in some basic ideas like safety in numbers. Studies show that if a large number of people in a group speak out against bullying, it's harder for a bully to find a specific target and they may even face social repercussions for trying. Our kids need to try and stay calm if they see a bullying situation. They need to use a powerful voice and body stance as they come into the interaction, and they need to do this in a public place. They can use humor to redirect the conversation or distract the focus of the bully. They can use a calm voice, look the bully in the eye, and use clear language like "Stop this. No one likes it." Let your kid practice with you, have them recite some of the things they'd want to say to the bully to make sure they are clear, concise, and calm.

Some schools of thought recommend documenting the bullying your child is experiencing or witnessing, because that list of transgressions can motivate them to action or back them up with an authority figure if they get in trouble for standing up to the bully. Your kid needs to know that they might need to use physical defenses, but they should use them as a last resort. Hopefully the correct intervention would happen before any bullying crosses that line, but having them be prepared to do so is important. And discuss the possible consequences for becoming physical at schools and other places they may be. And tell them what *your* expectations of them are. That is, if they defend themselves appropriately, are you going to advocate for them at school, even when they are then suspended for doing so?

Also, note that most of the information about bullying focuses on children bullying other children. Not adults bullying children. And not just the weirdo adults in line next to them at Family Dollar, but adults that have a level of power over their lives. The family member, teacher, pastor, or parent of a friend. Encourage them to tell you about everyone who contributes to them feeling like shit so you can help them parse out if there is a problematic adult in their life. If your kids are going about their lives, following your rules, and another adult has a problem with them? You want your kids to tell you and also politely tell the person in question to take it up with you and back off of them.

And teach them how to communicate in ways that won't get them in more trouble with those aforementioned individuals. Faith always told her kids to be the polite one, and let her do the heavier stuff, which, come to think of it, was the same advice she gave her clients when she was a court liaison case manager. In doing so, the power differential changes, and the bullying adult in question will learn to either pick on someone their own size or shut their piehole.

Faith's son was pretty boss when he told a school administrator "I'll turn my shirt inside out for the rest of the day because you feel it is inappropriate. However, my mom bought me this shirt and we both like it and I don't know that either of us would agree that it was in violation of the school dress code. Could you please call her to discuss your concerns?"

You can also start coaching them to politely question as they get older. Asking the meddling aunt, for example, "I'm not sure why you are commenting on my weight in a negative way. It feels unkind, is that your intent? I thought we were here for a birthday party, which is supposed to be a fun event." And the crap "jokes" people tell as a subtle form of bullying? A response that almost always works is "I don't get it, why is that funny?" puts the impetus back on the adult in question to explain themselves.

Finally, just let them know that you support them no matter what, and that standing up to a bully is an important part of your family culture of fostering kindness and respect in the world. We will raise children who are not bystanders, but calm ambassadors for peace.

How to Be Patient

Faith will let you know how to do this if she ever figures it out. Heh.

But seriously, we live in such a rage-quit society, it's no wonder that it's so difficult to find people who are built to put in the time and effort to complete a long-term project. I mean honestly, we carry tiny computers (that we sometimes use to make phone calls) with us at all times and have infinite human understanding available with the taps of a few buttons. But so much of what is really worthwhile should take time. Finishing school or job training. Making an authentic risotto. Falling truly in love.

Give your kids lessons of patience where they are able to see the payoff at the end. Faith did this back in the day when her kids wanted a Wii. We made it a household savings task where all extra change everyone had went into a jar until the money was raised. It took awhile, and her kids would inspect the jar hopefully. But they also liked the game of filling the jar, even picking up pennies in the parking lot to add. Y'all change-droppers funded their Wii, just saying. This is what teaches them the value of perseverance.

And if you suck at being patient? Y'all, we feel you. And we feel it's important to own that in our out-loud voices with our kids as something we are all working on. As in, "I hate waiting, too!

Let's figure out ways to be more patient together!" Or measure progress together or even just grumble about how much it sucks together. It can be good for us *and* be really difficult to do at the same time. For Bonnie, conversations with her daughter around patience typically focus on the idea that everyone is doing the best they can with what they've got. There's a long line at the drive-through? Be patient because everyone's working hard. There's empathy in patience, and kindness too, and those are two key values for Bonnie and her daughter.

That's all well and good when they are waiting for burgers or whatever, but Bonnie does seriously struggle to maintain any sense of composure when her kid is the one taking forever. How can you maintain patience with your kid when you've asked them fifty bazillion times to put on their shoes or feed the pets or take out the compost? Bonnie has tried a lot of strategies for this, and she's not sure she's found one that really works long-term. She has tried yelling (that's like, negative patience points so probably not that), cajoling (moves quickly to yelling, so probably not that), and even bribery (gets expensive quickly, so probably not that either). The thing that's worked the best so far is to give frequent reminders, like "We leave for school in twenty minutes and you need to be ready to go!" along with letting her kid deal with the natural consequences of her actions. If she doesn't do something on time, she's late to school (which she haaaaaates), or she's late to the birthday party and misses some of the fun, or she doesn't get to go with dad to the grocery store. That way, Bonnie can do less patience-losing and more conversations about decisions and their outcomes. Bonnie decided a long time ago that she doesn't like who she is when she yells and loses her temper, so she's done a lot of work around managing her activation levels with breaks or grounding techniques.

It's not your kids' job to be parentable. It is your job to parent them anyway. How can you change your approach to be a more patient parent to them? What can you do for yourself that helps you lose it less often?

Take Care of Yourself

Bonnie has learned that she's way more likely to be on edge, too tense, or too snippy if she hasn't had enough water. There's something about that "I'm a little too thirsty/maybe dehydrated" feeling that makes her feel really close to the edge. For Faith, it's low blood sugar. She's Admiral Hangry, remember? Every irritating situation will push her anger button until her internal thermometer tells her it's time to explode. When really, if she would just have a handful of almonds, her reaction would be to say, "Well, clean it up then" and move on.

Here's some feedback that Bonnie gives clients and it almost always annoys them, so she's gonna annoy you with it too: you must literally do the things you need to do to feel like a human. Drink water. Eat food. Get sleep. Move your body. See your friends.

Yes, you bought this book and some of the advice was "drink more water" and sorry not sorry because it's legit. You need basic care to feel your best. Sometimes, your best still feels crappy as hell, we know. And we know that more water and better nutrition won't fix things. But like, they do help, and give you some power to do the things within your control to change your outlook.

Our commitment to the work of parenting does not have to be (and shouldn't be) equal to our willingness to martyr ourselves. While that message may come through from society, the fact remains that none of us can pour from an empty cup. And if we are starting to feel drained, burned out, martyred . . . well, that makes us much more likely to lose our shit on people. As we say in Texas, "Get off the cross, honey, we need the wood."

Think about your own experiences with being parented. What model did your parents set for taking care of themselves? How do you take care of yourself now, and does it feel sufficient?

We have to take time to refill our own cups, so we can pour our love and attention out for others. If we are taking good care of ourselves, taking care of others becomes an act of love and can feel fulfilling and joyful. If we aren't, all that caring becomes a big ole chore, and nobody likes to feel like a chore. Faith and Bonnie both talk to a lot of clients who share with us the struggle of parenting, and sometimes losing our own identities in the fog of "I'm a parent and I have to give everything to my kids, and to take an afternoon to myself takes time away from them and that's selfish and maybe I'm supposed to be selfless and not need that time to myself." And as that perceived societal expectation of selflessness permeates parents' attempts to engage in self-care, they end up feeling selfish and guilty instead of recharged and refilled. We all deserve a chance to have a quiet moment, to disconnect and disengage, to know ourselves in our own ways and not just in parent ways.

Let's look at what it means to be selfish for a second. Being selfish in the traditional sense is a bad thing; it's egotistical, focusing primarily on your own gain or pleasure with no concern for others' needs or wellbeing. That's not what we are advocating for here. We are advocating for focusing on your needs and pleasures as a human with the end goal of being more present and open to the needs and wants of others in your life. By showing compassion toward yourself, you're making others' lives better, and that's definitely not selfish; that's in fact, the famous and elusive win-win scenario. You are being self-focused to have your needs met so you can then meet the needs of others. There is nothing shitty about that.

Calm Your Tits

We all know how we are *supposed* to be. And when we hit the point where we aren't operating from that place, we try to force our way through. Sometimes we *can't*. Not in the moment. At some point, we need a break. And our kids need a break from their hyper-reactive dickhead parent. You need to be aware of what sets you off, and how to recognize when you are getting set off so you can step away and regroup. If you can assign a pinch hitter, do so. Faith and her dear friends who helped her co-parent literally call each other or tap each other on the shoulder and say "Tag, you're it," and the relief parent comes up to bat.

If you're by yourself, that's okay too. Take a break and come back to the situation. For example, yes, we know we are supposed to comfort a crying baby, but if you are so activated by several hours of nonstop inconsolable colic, put the baby in a safe place and go take a shower. Run the vacuum cleaner to drown out the crying noise. Y'all's tenseness is feeding off of one another's and there is no consoling going on. Faith had zero problem doing that when her kiddos were teeny. When they were embiggened, she would say "I need for us to both go to our rooms and calm down a bit so we can come back to this in a better way."

Calm-down time is great to incorporate with other consequences or behavior plans. For example, Bonnie's daughter has always had a list of consequences for when she makes decisions that are not in line with those expected of her. The list was created when she was three, and has been adjusted slightly over time. It starts with the loss of a privilege and is followed by an age-appropriate timeout (between thirty seconds and two minutes, depending on the age of your kid and their abilities to sit still. Make this doable and winnable for them). If she can complete the timeout quietly and follow that with a respectful conversation about what happened, she can re-earn the privilege she lost. Bonnie created the process this way on purpose; it gives both her and the kid a break to collect thoughts, take some deep breaths, and try again. There are other consequences on the list, but Bonnie hardly ever has to advance to those because the calm-down break is a powerful reset for both of them.

So calm your tits! At least calm one of your tits. Bring that calm to activating situations and then try to *breathe* to keep the calm as long as you can. And when you can't anymore, take a break and calm your tits again.

Parenting While Managing Your Own Mental Health Issues

Bonnie and Faith are both therapists who have therapists. We know the value of having a place to process, get support, and work on our triggers and coping skills. Bonnie takes antidepressants, which she had to start the year her daughter was born, because holy shit, postpartum anxiety is real and debilitating. To do her best to be a functional parent instead of a wobbly mass of anxiety-goo, the meds and therapy are important additions to her overall self-care plans.

What's the status of your mental health currently? How does the way you feel emotionally or mentally affect you day-to-day? Do you feel you have the space and time you need to learn about yourself?

Think about your own experiences growing up. Did the adults in your life struggle with mental health? How would you have known if they did?

Many clients in session with Bonnie reflect on those questions and find that their parents' mental health did show up for them as kids even if they may not have had the words at the time. Sometimes it felt like a general funk through the house. Or maybe it was in the form of a parent who had a hard time getting out of bed or staying off substances. But other times it is more understated; a mom who loses her temper in a flash, or a dad who is quietly seething at a dinner table. Sometimes it is a feeling of "Some feelings weren't okay and I didn't know why."

Our parents and their parents didn't necessarily have the same views of mental health care that Gen-X and millenial parents do. Those generations didn't have the access to therapy or meds that we have now, and there was a hardcore stigma to needing or wanting those things anyway. That stigma persists in many communities and it may even be something you feel yourself. What messages did you get from your parents or grandparents about experiences with mental health?

If you have a mental health issue that interferes with your overall functioning, you know that managing it on a good day can be hard. You know that the exhaustion and stress of juggling all the parts of your own life can trigger mood changes, insomnia, substance-use, or even suicidal ideation. We talk with clients all the time who are extremely worried about the effects of their own mental health on their children and the people they love. Your mental health, like all health issues, deserves to be met with compassion and a comprehensive treatment plan.

Be proactive about creating the treatment plan you need in order to address your symptoms as thoroughly as possible. Do you need talk therapy, meds, inpatient treatment, weekly support groups? Is the treatment plan you're on now meeting your needs or does it need adjusting? We are living in unprecedented times; adjust your treatment as often as you need to help you keep up. If you need a place to start, we recommend connecting with your primary care provider. That's a person who likely knows your medical history and can support you in finding community resources and referrals to mental health care.

Using Current Events and Pop Culture as an Opening

We've mentioned this idea a few times throughout, but let's get into how to actually use pop culture as a way to start conversations with your kids. Pop culture is typically thought of as mass media and is most frequently aimed at younger people. That alone makes it prime conversation ground because it might be stuff you don't understand or that hasn't been directly marketed to you as a parent. You can scan websites or news to learn about the latest stuff and then sound really cool when you're like, "So I heard a story on NPR about TikTok and the ways it works to create community," and your kid will definitely roll their eyes at you—but it's easy to follow that up with some questions like "What do you like on TikTok? Have you learned anything interesting there? I heard there are some therapists on there teaching grounding techniques, that's pretty interesting!"

Movies and TV shows are reliable for these types of openings. Story lines are often written to have some reflection of real life, so it can open up conversations about presence or absence of diversity, use of tropes, discussing what happened versus what we would do in a situation, or the ways characters can be toxic, controlling, or even abusive. Try to stick with your handy-dandy open-ended questions so you avoid sounding boring or preachy:

- "What do you like about this show?

- What do you think about that character/story line/ scenario?

- Wow that was a major cliffhanger episode! What do you think will happen next?

- What do you like/dislike about the relationships in this movie?"

Nowadays, there are lots of shows that work hard to reflect current culture and relevant events. So using pop culture in this way can give you an in to talk about things like Black Lives Matter, abortion, politics, immigration, sex and consent, mass incarceration, poverty and classism, ableism, transphobia . . . choose your topic and find a show that can open up the conversation for you. That's why representation matters; so we can see ourselves in the stories we consume and we can carry away our own interpretations.

Pop culture is an interesting piece of discussions around mental health. There are lots of positive examples of people in TV, movies, or music experiencing mental health challenges or crises and dealing with them in constructive ways. There are also lots of controversial instances of this same idea. But any of these media examples can give you an opening to the discussion, because you can seem like you're just making simple conversation about something you saw on Netflix instead of overtly poking around in your kids' life. This gentle start-up approach reduces resistance to the conversation and gives space for hypotheticals, questions, concerns, and differing perspectives.

A different issue comes when these pop culture images start affecting our kids' internal sense of worth. We are living in a very visual world. Apps and online spaces rely heavily on visual media to drive traffic through the virtual world. Those images can be heavily altered, provocative, upsetting, or unrealistic. Your toddler putting a red towel on their head to be the Little Mermaid is adorable (and an Instagram gold mine). But it's worrisome when our kids get older and start to think they have to match their idols in literal ways that start causing body dysmorphia. All the body talk we do from the start is hugely important here, plus, this is where we add in discussion about the fact that their favorite stars and influencers are *paid to look that way*. Their favorite pop singer is adorable, yes, because it's her job to be adorable, her income is dependent on being adorable, and it costs a freaking fortune to be adorable. Simple statements like "Yes, she is super cute. I'm so glad my job doesn't require me to put hours of work into my appearance every day before leaving the house so I'm always camera ready! Looking that put-together all the time is a really hard job!" can really put those ideas into perspective.

The people in power see the potential of pop culture as well, for recruitment or general heart/mind influence. If you're actively using pop culture in the ways we describe here, make sure you're doing your own research about the source, and you're teaching young people how to separate entertertainment from propaganda. Critical thinking about the messages we get from pop culture is a valuable skill. And frankly, discussions where we dissect and critically review pop culture are some of Bonnie's favorite discussions. It's a fun way to frame and talk about serious things.

How to Raise Your Kid When You're Inside/Outside the Dominant Paradigm

We would wager that since you're here, you're already somewhat out of the dominant paradigm. You're here because you want a different world and you're rejecting some of the traditions and beliefs that got us here.

What is the dominant paradigm of family and parenting? It's the outdated 1950s version of family that doesn't serve our twenty-first century needs. It's cishet parents (a matched immutable binary set of one man and one woman, of course) and cishet kids, and probably everyone is white, and definitely everyone is neurotypical, and there's not a lot of space for variation.

Some of us are parenting in that space. Bonnie parents in that space; she's married to a cishet man and her daughter, so far at least, also meets that description. But that doesn't make their family any better or worse than other families, and that's the key idea of feminist parenting: make room for all kinds of families without arbitrarily deciding what is "normal" and create affirming spaces for all families.

If you're outside the dominant paradigm, you're probably already talking to your kids about it. They see differences and feel discrimination and have likely brought it up to you in some way. You've talked about code switching and other ways to stay safe, and you've worried about your kids in ways other parents haven't. Parenting is already heavy stuff; you've carried even more of the load. We hope that you have a good community of support from other parents outside the paradigm. And we hope some of those dominant-paradigm parents see what you're doing and work to take some of your load.

If you're in the dominant paradigm, your job is to disrupt it.

What about you or your family makes you different? Where are places or relationships in your life where those differences are celebrated? Or where those differences are seen as deficits? How are you disrupting the status quo and how can you bring more people to that disruption?

There is so much discussion currently about privilege and what that means. And for every discussion about the recognition of privilege, there is three times as much discussion pushing back against the idea. And privilege, in current discourse, is not "The founders of Halo Top raising seven figures of start-up capital from family and friends" type privilege. Chances are good you aren't reading this book if you have access to those kinds of family members and friends.

Privilege in this case means *the absence of barriers*. Stairs are not a barrier for anyone who doesn't use a wheelchair (or any other mobility support or who lives with a chronic pain condition). We don't float magically up them, but we are able to use our legs to move up them without causing harm to our bodies. And this is true of poverty, racism, colorism, sexism, heterosexism, cissexism, etc., etc.

We are trying to see, and help our kids see, things that are so pervasive they become invisible. We are not asking fish to watch for the shark. We are asking fish *to become aware of the ocean itself*. This is incredibly difficult and incredibly necessary for the creation of a better society.

This means teaching our kids to believe what other people tell us about their experiences of the world, and looking at the world through someone else's eyes to the extent that they can do so. How do we see the water and teach our kids to see the water? We start with the small things that we can do in the immediate present to give our kids a sense of accomplishment and purpose, like: "Wow, all these carts left all over the sidewalk would make it impossible for someone who uses a walker or is pushing their baby in a stroller to get through. Let's move them to the corral so they are out of the way."

You've just taught your kid to notice that how they maneuver around obstacles isn't possible for everyone. They are going to be less likely to leave their own cart on the sidewalk and make sure that others have as clear a path as possible.

Dismantling these structures when all we have is a plastic spoon is doable if we all start digging away chunks of the foundation with our individual spoons.

Co-Parenting Wokely

Okay, this is really, really difficult. Bonnie and Faith both do couples work, which is like standing in the middle of a bidirectional autobahn watching cars speed past you chaotically going in both directions. You're trying not to get hit and are supposed to maintain a calm demeanor in the process. And if we are navigating the ending of that relationship and deciding on co-parenting standards? Y'all we do *not* get paid enough. Faith has also had to co-parent after an unfun divorce, so has her own personal luggage in that area.

Which is all to say, this is really difficult. The co-parenting classes that judges order are usually pretty crappy. Your ex is weaponizing every fucking thing, and you are feeling painfully wounded and in your feels.

The best advice we can give is to do the right thing even when no one else is. I know it's not fair if your ex is showing their ass, but time bears all of that out in the end. It takes a while and it's a painful process, but it keeps your kiddos from having to choose sides in the present and gives them a level of stability to look back on. Some of the things that help:

1) Don't bad-mouth your ex. Even if they are trash and not in the fun Oscar-the-Grouch sense of the word. Let their relationship with your kids stand on its own, not be influenced by your relationship with them. Either they will be better to their kids (thank fuck) or demonstrate quite handily how trash they are. Either way, your kiddos' relationship with your ex should be their relationship, not yours.

2) Don't get triangulated into stuff. If your kiddo bad-mouths them or complains, turn that back toward their relationship with that parent whenever possible. Start with "Did you tell them you were uncomfortable with meeting the person they are dating? That sounds like a conversation the two of you should have." Obviously this doesn't apply to immediately dangerous situations like they were driven by your ex who was raging drunk behind the wheel, but absolutely applies to the tattley stuff kids do during a divorce to get a rise out of us. It doesn't mean accepting falsehood, however. If it is something along the lines of "Mom said you are a [fill in the blank with pejorative of your choice]" a

conversation-ending response would be "That's not a true statement."

3)   Keep the issues between you and your ex between you and your ex. Don't parentify your kids, don't make them the person you talk to about this shit. Go get 73 therapies if you need too, but don't make it your kids' job. The message your kids should hear should be some variation of "That's stuff between us and it's hard right now. But we are both your parents, both love you sososo much, and we are still a family even if we are no longer together. We are having to figure out how to do that well, and it's been hard, and it's taking more time than we want it to, thanks for being patient."

4)   Make preemptive rules with your ex about how certain things will be handled by both of you should they arise in the future. You can't plan for every contingency, and you can't make them act right, but you can act right and hope they will do the same. For example, you may think you are never going to date anyone ever again. And you may be right. But you may also change your mind. So a rule about how long someone new has to be in either of y'all's lives before they meet the kids is super important. And maybe even rules around how long before y'all tell each other/do you want to meet new partners before the kids do, etc. If you are doing 73 therapies right now, this is a good thing to strategize with your therapist about, since they know the specifics of your situation.

5) When all else fails, use the general therapy rule that all of Faith's clients hear at some point. And that is to do the best you can with the information you have right now. Or, to put in her tough-therapist voice, "Ten years from now, will you be embarrassed about what you're doing right now?" She doesn't want you to ever be upset at yourself for doing the best you can in any situation, but especially in an acrimonious breakup we feel very wounded and can behave in very wounding ways. So no matter how your ex is showing their ass, don't show yours. If you know better right now, and you know after the emotions have settled you'll recognize your behavior as shitty, don't do it. Future self will really be grateful to not need 73 more therapies to resolve that guilt.

Navigating Non-Woke Parental Figures

So you're woke as can be, but chances are there are other adults in your kids' lives that are parental-esque figures—whether it's an ex, a stepparent, a teacher, or relative, you're not the only adult they look up to. How can woke parents navigate that?

This book has included a lot of ideas and questions about conversations you'll want to have with your kids. So now we want to ask you: what conversations do you want/need to have with other adults in your life? You're educating yourself, you're empowering your kids, you're working toward progress and inclusivity . . . how will the other adults in your life react to your growth? You're woke; you see that things are not what you wish them to be for your kids and for all kids. It's very likely you have people in your life who will not agree with your viewpoints. That includes teachers, grandparents, co-parents . . . other people who have influence with your kids and that your kids likely look up to.

What boundaries do you feel you need in those relationships? For example, maybe it's okay for your mom to talk with you about politics, but you don't want her to talk about it in front of your kids. We determine our boundaries by paying close attention to our gut reactions and responses to the ways we interact with people. Who are the people in your life that give you a strong gut reaction? What ideas do they have that you struggle with or do not want your kids to engage with at this time?

These boundaries likely look different in each relationship in your life. And that's complicated, yes, but that's the work. You want to explore your wokeness and you want to create a safe space for your kids to explore what it means for them. So you have to identify the relationships where that's safe and productive and where it's not. Any adults that would use name-calling, boundary violation, coercion, or anger in these types of conversations need to know from the start that those behaviors aren't accepted in interactions with your kids. If that means these topics are off the agenda completely, then that's what it means. Your boundaries need to be communicated from the beginning and need to be enforced consistently. How will you respond when your boundaries are ignored or purposefully violated?

How do you want to communicate these boundaries to your kids? Do you want them to know you've had these conversations or not? How will the boundaries affect their relationships with the people in question?

It might be helpful to make a list of the relationships where you feel you need stronger boundaries. What boundaries do you need? How can you communicate them to the people involved? It might be as simple as a text message when you're on the way to a family dinner, "Please remember that we do not want to talk about politics at this family dinner. We are gathering to celebrate our dog's graduation from obedience school and we won't let the spotlight stray from her accomplishments."

You need some serious and uncomfortable conversations with these non-woke figures. The shame you've wrestled as you've worked through this process yourself will be fresh and strong in people who haven't been on your journey. Only you can do the risk/benefit analysis of setting these boundaries and maintaining those relationships. Your end goal is to keep your kids in a place that's emotionally safe for them to continue to explore what progressive ideas mean for them without feeling like they are a disappointment to any of the adults they admire.

Navigating "Parenting" Kids That Aren't Yours

Whether it's your kid's best friend, your friend's kid, etc., you're going to run into other kids who look up to you. How do you navigate upholding your values (especially if *your* kid is right there) without alienating their parents? There are a couple different issues here. One is the kiddos you have a parental-type relationship with (cuz whoever their bio and/or legal parents are, they agreed to you being in their lives, or, they don't have any viable parent-people—bonus kids).

Then, there are just "other people's kids." Your kiddo's friend who is spending the weekend with y'all and keeps harassing the dog and is in desperate need of correction. Now, Faith grew up in the '70s and '80s. And on military bases. If you were at someone else's house and acted a fool, their momma would spank your butt and send you home. And as you walked in the door, *your* momma would be hanging up the phone with an "I see, thanks for telling me, we'll take care of it." And then you got your butt spanked again. At least by your momma, and maybe a third time when your daddy got home. And because Faith was a sassy-mouthed little urchin, this probably explains why her butt is so flat to this day.

And that doesn't happen anymore. Clearly for the better. But that made it easier to navigate, at least. Behavior expectations didn't change based on whose kid was in the house. Rules were rules. Now we gotta have the convo. And honestly, whether they are an all-in bonus kiddo or one of the neighborhood pack raiding your popsicle stash, being in contact with the parent-people with the actual legal standing in their lives is really important.

If it is a kiddo new to your abode, ask the dropping-off parent-person straight out. "Hey your kiddo is probably way better behaved than my weirdo, but if there is anything I need to bring up to them cuz our house rules may be a little different, how do they best hear stuff? Is there anything I need to be aware of that they struggle with? Anything in particular you need to hear back about or anything you want to handle yourself?" The best part of all this is that all kiddos will then know that all adults are a united front on expectations and they can't get sneaky.

As it becomes a kiddo that you are especially close to (a full-on bonus kiddo), that role may get more fluid with their parents-of-record, but communication is still important. Even if it's a brief convo, more of an FYI, "This came up today and it's totally already been addressed by . . ."

If there is a longer-term behavior or personality challenge, then we're getting back into the area we discussed before regarding the friend of Faith's older child, the one with some problematic viewpoints. We can't set boundaries for other people, only for ourselves. So that particular friend wasn't invited into Faith's home (Faith's boundary) rather than Faith having a smackdown with them over values and political symbolism and other stuff that was not her place to get into. And as mentioned before, Faith explained to Kid One that she wants everyone to feel safe in her home, and their friend's behavior would challenge that safety for other people which makes it not acceptable.

Learning from Your Kids

Things will change—quickly—and what's acceptable today will be realized as problematic tomorrow. That's progressivism; there's no finish line and the language and activism are fluid to reflect that reality. If you raise your kids right, they'll learn these things on their own, possibly before you do. So when they correct you, which they inevitably will, how will you respond? It's our job to accept these corrections and evolutions with grace and openness. The process is not a one-way, top-down distribution of information; it's a feedback loop based in equity and curiosity. We are building the scaffolding, remember? But we are building it so our kids can take over and build it even better, even more progressive, even more ideal.

When this happens, try "That's an interesting idea and different from what I was taught about this subject. What does this mean to you? Help me understand where it came from so I can learn more about this idea right along with you!"

Or "When I learned about this a few years ago, we talked about it in another way. I love that some new ideas are coming around on this topic. Tell me more!"

Or how about "What are you passionate about on this topic?"

Or even "I think of this word like 'this' and it sounds like you think of it like 'that.' Help me understand the differences here. I want to learn more about your understanding of this!"

Because we are all coming from an imperfect background, we can all identify places we wish we'd acted differently, been more (or less) vocal, done more research, or generally just done better. It's possible your kids will have questions about those decision points. If we are to be honest about our growth and learning, it means we have to be welcoming of these call-ins. Put aside your defensiveness and do some processing of your own shame that comes from being part of the system. There are plenty of times feminism got it wrong: centering white women, excluding trans women, demonizing sex workers . . . there's a long list of places feminism has had a chance to evolve. It has evolved because people started questioning. When your kids start questioning, are you ready to learn and evolve along with them?

It's Never Too Late

A key piece of feminism is hopefulness; if we don't feel hopeful, then what are we working for? Feminism is the compassionate belief that we can see something unjust and work together to correct it. We are here to tell you, even if your kid has their own collection of red MAGA hats, there is hope for them yet.

Bonnie has joked for a long time that the only way her kid can really rebel is to register as a conservative when it's time for her to vote. Any other rebellions, Bonnie is confident she can weather, but to watch her kid take such an active stance against progress would be very difficult. To watch our kids take the path of the alt-right, the white supremacists, the "lock her up" chanters . . . that's seriously scary and difficult for parents to watch.

Who are the people most likely to be drawn into a phenomenon like QAnon? Studies show they are people who are prone to conspiracy theories already (e.g., 9/11 truthers or Obama birth certificate claims). They have signs of a persecution complex (everyone is out to get them or keep them from prosperity). They have strong associations of right and wrong and want to see bad guys lose. There's a clear presentation of the idea that there are people in power and they have secrets; people who get involved love the idea that those people will be exposed and a wrong will be righted. To be fair, those are enticing ideas; feminism likes ideas like that too. Right? We want to disrupt patriarchy and white supremacy and we want equitable distribution of power. The key difference is these phenomena are well-documented whereas the Q conspiracies are just that: conspiracies.

There are lots of places online where these factors are very purposefully used in a way that recruits people to alt-right beliefs. It can come from people researching vaccines, looking for relationship advice, trying to understand the economy, investigating Big Pharma, vague implications that children aren't safe . . . when algorithms are arranged correctly, people can follow myriad topics deep into conspiracies that lead to Q. And because the recruitment is so all-encompassing, there's not really a wide-scale way to deradicalize people.

So, what to do? Deradicalization is possible. The human mind is malleable and open to influence in it's need for connection, which is how people get radicalized, yes, but it's also the way we can reverse that. Look for people in your kid's life who can be a positive influence, someone who can tell affirming stories to your kid and bring them back from the brink. That may be a teacher, friend, therapist, or even some of the people online who are deradicalized themselves and do the work to help others get out of the movement. You hold the hope that change is possible, and then ask for the help you need to make that change possible.

White nationalism and the alt-right thrive by engaging people who feel victimized, misunderstood, or lonely. There are infinite on-ramps into the culture; searching for "depression" on YouTube will give you a stream of alt-right speakers talking about self-improvement, which will then lead you slowly down a rabbit hole toward extremism. Whatever the search, there's an answer somewhere online that leads to the alt-right. The movement uses propaganda and online communities to skillfully move people slowly toward extremism. Because it moves slowly, people are less likely to feel the cognitive dissonance that comes with extreme beliefs; it's a slow boil fueled by anger and fear, and the conspiracies incrementally start to feel true. The propaganda is used to isolate people from their families and friends in order to play up that feeling of loneliness, and then connects the targets to a group of other lonely people. This sense of finding belonging in a community is powerful and is often the main hurdle in getting someone away from extremism. Online, new recruits have a chorus of affirming and welcoming people to meet them. If they are missing that in their day-to-day life, it's tantalizing and addictive.

While getting involved in these communities seems welcoming and affirming, it's also incredibly lonely. As people get deeper in the conspiracy, they push away key support systems in real life. They lose the ability to find pleasure in things they once loved because they see the bad, the corruption, in every aspect of life.

It can be very sad to watch someone you love get drawn into that space.

If you're trying to get your kid back from the alt-right brink, you'll be tempted to move quickly or be forceful . . . because you're scared. But that approach will awaken their feelings of rebellion and can drive them further into the cause. Move slowly, gather a group of people who know your kid outside of the alt-right, and be prepared to be affirming and welcoming. Give what the online recruiters are giving, but add love. Move slowly to decrease resistance and the cognitive dissonance that happens when people are moving through ideologies.

Mike Rothschild, who writes extensively on QAnon, recommends not arguing ideological talking points but maintaining connection. In very basic "I'm going to the store, need anything?" kind of ways. He also encourages conversations that avoid fact-checking or mockery. That's tough because some of the ideas are straight-up bananas, but if you can be neutral in these times, you might be a person they trust when they want to get away from the group.

Everyone who talks openly about leaving a cult or the alt-right talks about a time when they had doubts; a claim was too outlandish or they were asked to give up something too important. Rothschild refers to those times as "dangling threads in a tapestry." Gently help your person find those loose threads and start slowly to pull on them. People who get out carry those doubts quietly. At some point, they had a conversation with a safe person who agreed with those doubts and held space for them to process through them.

Remember when you learned about the Holocaust for the first time? The horror you felt at the cruelty and atrocities committed?

Bringing someone out of extremism means they have to face that feeling of "If the Holocaust is real, then people are monsters," all over again. Those facts may be too ugly to face all at once, and that's why you've got to be persistent, but pace yourself. To come back from the alt-right means grappling with humanity's history and our own place within it.

There are lots of stories online of people who are deradicalized terrorists, white supremacists, or cult members. People do escape these terrible groups and ideas, but it takes patience and connection. Eli Saslow's book, *Rising Out Of Hatred*, is the story of white supremicist (and godson of David Duke) Derek Black's journey into healing. He said that picking apart his assumptions and where they came from was the first step, and the second was (once again) always choosing the option that didn't hurt people.

And he said his work came from people loving him for his personhood while challenging his belief system. He has reiterated over the years it wasn't exposure to differing ideas that did it, it was *people* who invited him in and included him while not becoming silent (and therefore complicit) around his beliefs.

It didn't happen until he was in college, around people who *didn't* think like him and his family and who were also willing to invest in the deep relational labor of loving someone through their journey out of hatred. Which brings back the point that having our children be exposed to a multitude of ideas early on improves their empathy and widens their thinking.

A kid who has radicalized isn't a cute Alex P. Keaton with a photo of Ronald Regan in his room. It's a different story right now. And if you are responsible for them and they are a minor living under your roof and with your support, you are well within your rights to set boundaries on their online behavior. If they are older, they are free to investigate whatever ideas speak to them, but we hope they will be able to reconnect with you once they are disillusioned with the movement.

CONCLUSION

Fun fact: Conclusions in books are not generally the last thing written. But in this case it was, because Bonnie and Faith struggled with this book. Not just because writing is hard (the process of writing sucks, having written something is the fun part). But because we struggle with our own enough-ness as parents. While we are passionate about the idea of bringing activism, feminism, and intersectionality into parenting, we both are not-so-secretly afraid that there is a far more parenty parent out there that should be writing it.

The process of working on this book has been years in the making. We were writing it in the stolen moments between clients. Early Sunday mornings before anyone else was awake. During elections and insurrections and protests and Supreme Court confirmations. Writing while trying to be present partners and loving parents and healthy therapists and savvy business owners. And we live in Texas so there's just a lot of general fuckery to contend with.

All that to say, we are frazzled. And if we are left in charge then wrong advice will be given, critical topics will get missed, and the microwave popcorn will definitely get burned. And honestly who gives their kids microwave popcorn anyway? It's full of diacetyl!

Writing this was a beautiful and collaborative process, but even with that overarching feeling, every time Bonnie sat down to write, she had to convince herself that she had something to say that people would actually want to read. There have got to be tons of parents out there doing it better than she is, right?

But imperfection is a huge part of this process for all of us. We're all striving to know better so we can do better. And writing this book is our way of living our imperfection and growth out loud. To encourage others to keep doing the same. All of us progressive parents, both book authors and book readers, are in a continuous process of trying to make the world a better place. And we need to not be fearful of sharing our voices, our visions, and our hard-won achievements in the process.

Which is all just to say, if this type of parenting feels overwhelming to you? Same team. But let's not let our imperfections and imposter syndrome keep us from talking about what's important and striving for progress. Because that's our goal, right? Being progressive parents, not perfect ones.

RESOURCES: MEDIA CONSUMPTION FOR THE WOKE PARENT AND CHILD

————————

For Parents and Kids of a Variety of Ages

Rad Dad (formerly a zine, now an anthology co-published by PM Press and Microcosm Publishing)

Hip Mama (hipmamazine.com, only online as of this writing)

East Village Inky (still in print, Ayun Halliday*[1] has an Etsy shop for subscriptions and back issues)

And Baby Makes More: Known Donors, Queer Parents, and Our Unexpected Families by Susan Goldberg et al.

PM Press in general publishes a *ton* on radical parenting, and they have killer deals when you order directly from them, like fifty percent–off sales pretty regularly. Because Jeff Bezos doesn't need our money.

A Mighty Girl: found at www.amightygirl.com is an extensive collection of diverse media for all age groups

Look for social media pages for minority-owned businesses in your area or that will ship to you. For example, San Antonio-Austin has a Facebook Group for Black-owned businesses called For The Culture that is mostly restaurants and catering. Social Distance Powwow Marketplace, also on Facebook, is all handmade goods by indigenous makers in the U.S. and Canada (Turtle Island!).

Trauma-Proofing Your Kids: A Parent's Guide To Instilling Confidence, Joy And Resilience by Peter Levine, PhD, and Maggie Kline

Books by Tim Tingle* for children, youth, and adults on both earlier and modern indigenous culture (focusing mostly on Choctaw culture)

The Trans Generation by Ann Travers

Tear Soup by Pat Schwiebert and Chuck DeKlyen

For Older Kids and Parents:
The Cooking Gene by Michael Twitty*

Young reader's versions of both Howard Zinn's *A People's History of the United States* and Roxanne Dunbar-Ortiz's *An Indigenous*

1(*) All asterisk people are people that Faith knows either slightly through social media or is an irl friend of hers.

Peoples' History of the United States (adapted by Dr. Jean Mendoza and Dr. Deb Reese⋆).

Tiny Beautiful Things by Cheryl Strayed

So You Want To Talk About Race by Ijeoma Oluo

Uncomfortable Conversations with a Black Man by Emmanuel Acho

How to Be an Anti-Racist by Ibram X. Kendi (has self-guided journal out now too)

Bad Feminist by Roxane Gay

Renée Watson's book for youth and teens (*Some Places More Than Others* and *Watch Us Rise* are probably Faith's faves)

Tribal Nations Maps by Aaron Caparella⋆

The Body Is Not an Apology by Sonya Renee Taylor

How the Word is Passed: A Reckoning with the History of Slavery Across America by Dr. Clint Smith

Poet X by Elizabeth Acevedo

Felix Ever After by Kacen Callender

I Wish You All The Best by Mason Deaver

Cemetery Boys by Aiden Thomas

Pet by Akwaeke Emezi

Younger Children

Inside Out (great characterization of emotions, Dr. John Schinnerer⋆ was a consultant on this Pixar film).

Red: A Crayon's Story by Michael Hall

I Am Jazz by Jessica Herthel and Jazz Jennings

My New Mommy by Lilly Mossiano

My New Daddy by Lilly Mossiano

Sometimes Mommy Gets Angry by Bebe Moore Campbell

Sparkle Boy by Leslea Newman

A is for Activist by Innosanto Nagara

A Day in the Life of Marlon Bundo by Jill Twiss

More by Dr. Faith

Books

The Autism Relationships Handbook (with Joe Biel)

Coping Skills

How to Be Accountable (with Joe Biel)

This Is Your Brain on Depression

Unfuck Your Adulting

Unfuck Your Anger

Unfuck Your Anxiety

Unfuck Your Blow Jobs

Unfuck Your Body

Unfuck Your Boundaries

Unfuck Your Brain

Unfuck Your Cunnilingus

Unfuck Your Grief

Unfuck Your Friendships

Unfuck Your Intimacy

Unfuck Your Worth

Unfuck Your Writing (with Joe Biel)

Woke Parenting (with Bonnie Scott)

Workbooks

Achieve Your Goals

The Autism Relationships Workbook (with Joe Biel)

How to Be Accountable Workbook (with Joe Biel)

Unfuck Your Anger Workbook

Unfuck Your Anxiety Workbook

Unfuck Your Body Workbook

Unfuck Your Boundaries Workbook

Unfuck Your Intimacy Workbook

Unfuck Your Worth Workbook

Unfuck Your Year

Other

Boundaries Conversation Deck

How Do You Feel Today? (poster)

Zines

The Autism Handbook (with Joe Biel)

The Autism Partner Handbook (with Joe Biel)

BDSM FAQ

Dating

Defriending

Detox Your Masculinity (with Aaron Sapp)

Emotional Freedom Technique

The Five Emotional Hungers

Getting Over It

How to Find a Therapist

How to Say No

Indigenous Noms

Relationshipping

The Revolution Won't Forget the Holidays

Self-Compassion

Sex Tools

Sexing Yourself

STI FAQ (with Bonnie Scott and Aaron Sapp)

Surviving

This Is Your Brain on Addiction

This Is Your Brain on Grief

This Is Your Brain on PTSD

Unfuck Your Consent

Unfuck Your Forgiveness

Unfuck Your Mental Health Paradigm

Unfuck Your Sleep

Unfuck Your Stress

Unfuck Your Work

Vision Boarding

Woke Parenting #1-6 (with Bonnie Scott)

ABOUT THE AUTHORS

Faith G. Harper, PhD, LPC-S, ACS, ACN is a bad-ass, funny lady with a PhD. She's a licensed professional counselor, board supervisor, certified sexologist, and applied clinical nutritionist with a private practice and consulting business in San Antonio, TX. She has been an adjunct professor and a TEDx presenter, and proudly identifies as a woman of color and uppity intersectional feminist. She is the author of the book Unf*ck Your Brain and many other popular zines and books on subjects such as anxiety, depression, and grief. She is available as a public speaker and for corporate and clinical trainings.

Bonnie Scott, MS, MA, LPC, is a professional therapist in private practice in San Antonio, TX. Born and raised in Texas and New Mexico, she is a staunch ally to the LGBTQ community and sits on the Board of Directors for Thrive Youth Center, an emergency shelter and housing program for LGBT youth in Texas. She works hard to be an intersectional feminist, generally striving to stir up good trouble in the world. She is passionate about her kid, her cats, her books, and her profession.